Up, Up and Away

Hello!

NORWICH

Edited by Lynsey Hawkins

First published in Great Britain in 2000 by
YOUNG WRITERS
Remus House,
Coltsfoot Drive,
Peterborough, PE2 9JX
Telephone (01733) 890066

HB ISBN 0 75432 264 5
SB ISBN 0 75432 265 3

FOREWORD

This year, the Young Writers' Up, Up & Away competition proudly presents a showcase of the best poetic talent from over 70,000 up-and-coming writers nationwide.

Successful in continuing our aim of promoting writing and creativity in children, our regional anthologies give a vivid insight into the thoughts, emotions and experiences of today's younger generation, displaying their inventive writing in its originality.

The thought, effort, imagination and hard work put into each poem impressed us all and again the task of editing proved challenging due to the quality of entries received, but was nevertheless enjoyable. We hope you are as pleased as we are with the final selection and that you continue to enjoy *Up, Up & Away Norwich* for many years to come.

CONTENTS

Colby School

Mulbarton Middle School

Jenny Michell Revell	54
Sarah Wyatt	54
James Stickland	55
Claire Ashby	56
Duncan Lloyd Baker	56
Sarah Mayhew	57
Matthew Newson	57
Abby Kirk	58
Jay Baker	59
Jenna Clarke-Frary	59
Kirsty Barrett	60
Jenny Bradley	60
Lawrence Burton	61
Brian Mills	61
Ben Shearing	62
Pip Morgan	63
Sam Catton	63
Morgan Williams	63

Notre Dame Prep School

Nathan Goose	64
Emma Lusher	64
Amy Holmwood	65
Meike Eliza Yallop	65
Madelaine Coutinho	66
Bryony Stanley	66
Zoë Tipler	67
Laura Sheppeck	68
Matthew Adlard	68
Roxanne Mitchell	69
Katrina Chia	70
Nicola Shattock	70
Joseph Malpas	71
Joshua Pond	71
Megan Groen	72

Samuel Tawn	72
James Brown	73
Anandi Green	73
Florence John	74
Jimmy Wheeler	74
Michael Saunders	75
Rebecca Thouless	76
Georgia Levell	76
Bethany Richards	77
Lisa Carroll	78
Jenny Sheppeck	78
Ben Meen	79
Camilla Brake	79
Rosie Black	80
Eloise Petzold	80
Susannah Ramjeet	81
Oliver Mortham	82
Hannah Donaldson-Davidson	83
Joshua Middleton	84
Bethany Flatt	84
Rachel Holden	85

Reepham Primary School

Catherine Cutts	86
Laura Jarvis	86
Jade Hardesty	87
Lizzy Carey	87
Rachel Stringer	88
James Harden	88
Danielle Laye	89
Theo Gadalla	89
Daisy Hood	90
Matthew Saunders	90
Sarah Warren	91
Sophie Watterson	92
Robert Jones	92

Seething & Mundham School

The Poems

THE HOLOCAUST

Hell's angels coming for her collection,
Sadly she is one of their selection.
The fiery pits of death and destruction,
At least that was her deduction.
Never-ever wandering free,
Never-ever being she.
Was she ever here or there,
Was she really anywhere?
Will she, was she ever her,
Or was it always just a blur.
Did she ever arrive at her station,
Did she ever reach her destination?
Then we realised it could be done,
But it was too late, she'd already gone!

Elizabeth Herbert (11)
Antingham & Southrepps CP School

BRAMBLE

A softy silky coat,
A star, a blaze
A long thick tail and a short thick mane.
She loves to jump,
She loves to eat carrots,
Apples, polos, lush grass
And hay
She loves to gallop across sunlit meadows.
She's a dark, dark bay.
She's a beautiful pony called Bramble.

Natalie Chubbock (11)
Antingham & Southrepps CP School

DON'T BLAME ME!

'It wasn't me Miss
I wouldn't dare lick Laura
I gave her a kiss.'

'Charlie hit me Miss!'
'Him again, Charlie don't hit!'
'It wasn't me, Miss.'

'Miss! Charlie kicked me.'
'I didn't Miss, she's lying!'
'Charles, look at her knee.'

So maybe I kicked
And gave her a small hitting
But she did it first!

Naomi Care (11)
Antingham & Southrepps CP School

WHAT IS WHITE?

What is white? Snow is white
Falling down right on this night.

What is beige? Paper is beige
As I write upon this page.

What is blue? The sky is blue
To make it nice for you.

What is green? Grass is green
And it can be seen.

Sophie Reed (9)
Antingham & Southrepps CP School

A RIDDLE

I love being wet
But I'm never cold
You can find me in school
Until I'm quite old.

My skin is so smooth
Because I've no hair
I dance in the sea
And I leap in the air.

I can jump through a hoop
And chatter like mad
I love all my family
My mum and my dad.

I can stand on my tail
And walk on the sea
I'm not really a fish
So what can I be?

The sea is my home
Where else can I be
Riding a bow wave
And dancing with glee?

Jessica Elliott (9)
Antingham & Southrepps CP School

HAIKU

There is a flower
There is a flower all bright
Shining in the sun.

Daisy Whitehead (9)
Antingham & Southrepps CP School

HAIKU

A spring Haiku
Flower opens in the sun
Hares fighting in lush meadows
Ice melts in sunlight.

A summer Haiku
Dragonfly near pond
Butterfly on a red bush
Eagle hunts a mouse down.

An autumn Haiku
Cold air claims the warmth
Chestnuts fall to cold ground
Winter's grasp is swift.

Jason Black (11)
Antingham & Southrepps CP School

CHESTNUTS AND CONKERS

Please don't pick us off the tree
We are nature, can't you see.
Conkers, chestnuts, all around,
Until next year, please leave us be
Then we'll begin to shoot you see,
And grow into a brand new tree.

Tom Patrickson (9)
Antingham & Southrepps CP School

THE GETAWAY DRIVER

The getaway driver zooms down the road,
The getaway driver's in high speed mode!
The getaway driver is in pursuit,
The getaway driver has got all the loot.

The getaway driver drives through the drain,
The getaway driver gets caught in the rain.
The getaway driver speeds through the mall
And everyone's annoyed, one and all.

The getaway driver gets rammed in the back.
The getaway driver shouts 'I'll get you for that!'
The getaway driver has the cops in a tiff
The getaway driver hangs over a cliff.

William John Grey (11)
Antingham & Southrepps CP School

MONDAY'S MOUSE

Monday's mouse is fluffy and grey
Tuesday's mouse stuck in the hay
Wednesday's mouse is not up to be fed
Thursday's mouse is going to be wed
Friday's mouse is very greedy
Saturday's mouse is doing her weeding
And the mouse that was born on the seventh day -
Well, we lost him, is that okay?

Elizabeth Lovick (9)
Antingham & Southrepps CP School

WHAT AM I?

I am black and white
Sometimes I give people a fright
And only come out at night.
I am sometimes found,
Underground
And I don't make much noise
When I play with boys.
I live in a set
And I'm not a pet.

A: A badger

Matthew Baker (10)
Antingham & Southrepps CP School

WHAT IS?

What is white? Snow is white
Falling down like a white kite.

What is green? Leaves are green
Sitting like a pretty queen.

What is yellow? A lemon is yellow
Juicy, ripe and mellow.

Anna Elizabeth Brown (10)
Antingham & Southrepps CP School

1 x 1

2 x 2 I haven't got a clue
3 x 3 I've hurt my knee
4 x 4 I'm down on the floor
5 x 5 my plant is alive
6 x 6 I'm making a mix
7 x 7 I'm going to Heaven
8 x 8 I'm walking very straight
9 x 9 I'm feeling very fine
10 x 10 I've got a new red hen
11 x 11 the secret seven
12 x 12 I can see a little elf.

Emma Tilbury & Laura Rose (8)
Antingham & Southrepps CP School

HABITATS

A grazing marsh is many meadows
Home to birds and cattle herds
The water of the Broads is dirty
But loved by ducks and geese and birds
Now Fens are like a patchwork quilt
With sedge and reeds to shelter birds
But the snail wins the Habitat Trophy
His shell is his home and his own.

William Terry (10)
Antingham & Southrepps CP School

ME

If I could be a dog, I would be a
Cocker spaniel being gently tickled
By my owner.

If I could be an item of clothing,
I would be a warm fleece,
Cuddly and fresh from the wash.

If I were a car, I would be an old
VW Beetle, speeding down the main road
As fast as my engine would go.

If I were a flower, I would be a sunflower,
Big and bright, letting the sun's rays
Absorb into my skin.

Katja McKinlay (12)
Bignold Middle School

WHAT IS PURPLE?

Purple is a dizzy feeling,
A flower shining with all its might
Purple is mother's eye-shadow glistening,
A mythical fish in the big sea, swimming away,
A cool punkman's hairdo sticking up!
Purple is a beautiful amethyst round a girl's neck
A summer twilight sky!

Rachel Bedder (8)
Bignold Middle School

PLAYTIME

Some children stay in and hide
All the rest rampage outside
As the children run around
The playground echoes with their sound.

You can hear the noise of approaching cars
And children jumping off the monkey bars
You hear the slaps as they land on their feet
And the rustle of packets as others begin to eat.

There is a thud as a ball hits the wicket
In a match of *kwik* cricket
A basketball hits the rim with a clunk
As Jack Moore does a 'slam dunk'.

Then,
The whistle blew
The children flew
The doors closed
And pencils started scratching.

Josh Saunders (11)
Bignold Middle School

WHAT IS BLUE?

Blue is sad
Blue is the sea, wavy and salty
Blue can be dark
The night of the day
Blue is a funeral, sad and moany
Blue is a song of sadness!

Isaac Peel (9)
Bignold Middle School

WHAT IS BLUE?

Blue is a sad face
A face with tears pouring
Blue is the sea
Crashing on the rocks
A sapphire is blue
Shining in the sun
Blue is frost
On a cold, cold day
Blue is the colour of my eyes
Blue is the colour of my tears.

Alice Grenville (9)
Bignold Middle School

WHAT'S IT LIKE?

The sun is like a burning light bulb
Lighting up space
An ice-cream is like the North Pole
Freezing any life-forms.
The old tree is like an elderly person
Wrinkling through the years.
A train is like a bullet
Speeding to a distant destiny.
A frog is like a leapfrog tournament
Squeezed into one reptile.

Jack Allen (9)
Bignold Middle School

PARENTS

Parents like you
to;
Keep out of their way when they're busy,
eat your greens,
keep clean,
eat your dinner.

Parents like you
to;
Get up in the morning,
turn off the TV,
work hard at school,
keep your desk clean.

Parents like you
to;
Wear clean clothes in the morning,
not put them in an Old People's Home
when they're old,
make your own sandwiches,
clean up after yourself.

Parents like you
to;
Dust around the room
water the plants,
not laze around,
and do the washing-up.

Parents like you to . . .
make the tea!

Fiona Clark (9)
Bignold Middle School

SPRING DAYS

Springy green grass
The winter has passed!

The sun is shining
No more lightning
No more snowing
Animals growing.

Springy green grass
The winter has passed

Out in the sun
Lots of fun
Come on let's run
It's spring everyone!

Springy green grass
The winter has passed.

Georgina Ball (9)
Bignold Middle School

WHAT IS GREEN?

Green is gecko, small and scared,
Or it could be a forest, wet and shaded.
Green is the tree that I always climb,
Green is a sign that tells me to go,
Green is a way of life!

Jasper Dumas (8)
Bignold Middle School

PLAYGROUND SOUNDS

Children in the playground
Rumble, crunch, scatter.
Children munch their lunches
While they sit and natter.

Girls sitting in the corner
Counting out their cash
Boys having races
Dash, dash, dash.

Dinner ladies blow their whistles
Children start to crowd,
Everyone blocks their ears
As they are that loud.

Cars zoom past the gate
Honk, honk, beep, beep,
One goes past quite quickly
The children start to leap.

Just before the whistle goes
A final goal is scored,
Everyone's gobsmacked
They gasped and they roared.

It's quarter past one
The final whistle blows,
'It's time to go in' they shout
The playground's filled with 'Oh nos.'

We are lining up and it's time
This poem came to a close,
The children have grumpy faces,
They stopped. They thought. They froze.

Emma Copsey (12)
Bignold Middle School

PARENTS

Parents like you to;
clean your pets out and feed them,
eat your vegetables,
have manners
and always say please.

Parents like you to;
tidy your room if a friend is coming round
and don't play rough,
always say thank you.

Parents like you to;
be neat all of the time,
wake up in the morning nice and early,
so we will be on time for school.

Parents like you to;
go to bed without a fuss,
I just go along with her
and get ready for bed.

Parents like you to;
eat and do things you sometimes don't want to
but you will always . . .
love them.

Isabelle Francis (8)
Bignold Middle School

SPRING DAYS

Bulbs growing
Newborn lambs
Easter eggs
Leaves appearing.

Sun shining
Birds singing
Sharp showers
Lighter clothes.

Eva Palser (8)
Bignold Middle School

IF

If I was a dog
I'd be a golden Labrador
Trustful and reliable
And not too big.

If I was a flower
I'd be a dandelion
Harmless and interesting
With traces of colour.

If I was some clothing
I'd be a T-shirt
Useful and reliable
And easy to wear.

If I was a car
I'd be a Volvo
Working and useful
Going on and on.

But my mum says
That if I was a flower
I'd be a snowdrop
Colourful and pretty
A promise of things to come.

Khalid Hussin (12)
Bignold Middle School

PLAYGROUND SOUNDS

Time to go
Go out to play
In the playground sounds are heard
Teachers talking
People walking
Children laughing
Balls bouncing
Dogs barking
Cars starting
The whistle has been blown
Off we go
Back to work.

Alie Najjar (12)
Bignold Middle School

WHAT IS RED?

Red was the colour of Boudicca's hair
Red is fire
Waiting for the fire engine,
Red is my face
When I feel anger,
Red is a warning of danger!
Red is blood
Coming from injured people,
Red is a juicy, red tomato,
Waiting to be eaten by me!
Red is a tiger,
Hunting in the jungle.

Thomas Edwards (9)
Bignold Middle School

BOOKS

J K Rowling is in the garden writing Harry Potter 4
While R L Stine is drinking wine on his lino floor.
J Eldridge is getting info about the war
While Dick King Smith is writing more and more.
Robert Swindell chopping kindle to make a smoking fire
Michael Colman rising higher and higher.
Christopher Golden makes Buffy richer and richer
Alan Garner writes exciting stories with brilliant pictures.
Enid Blyton writing Famous Five books for the kids
While Terry Deary writes horrid history about the past.
Robin Jarvis with the great old spookies
Thomas Rockwell making money everywhere.
Jamie Rix writes funny tales for the kids
Shakespeare shining in the sky.
Michael Cox has the knowledge
Gillian Cross makes us scared of the headmaster.

Dominic Hogg (11)
Bignold Middle School

WHAT IS BLUE?

Blue is cold like the Titanic in the water,
People frozen!
Blue is the whale splashing in the dark ocean,
Blue is like the sky,
With bluebirds flying through the clouds,
Blue is the colour of people's eyes,
Born from a human.

Meryl Hammerton (8)
Bignold Middle School

WHAT IS BLUE

Blue is the sky way up high
Blue is the ocean down below
Blue are the bluebells in the spring
Blue is the carpet in my classroom
Blue is my pen scratching on my paper.

Debbee Norman (10)
Bignold Middle School

WHAT IS RED?

Red is a box with all my toys in,
A ruby with sparkly corners,
Red is a margin in a school book,
A red jumper that my friend wears,
An apple just about to come off the tree,
Red is the head of a parrot!
Red is a sign of danger!

Andrew Woodcock (8)
Bignold Middle School

WHAT IS WHITE?

White is soft like snow,
White like the morning clouds,
It could be a seagull dancing
In the gusting wind,
White is like the night stars.

Salsabil Morrison (8)
Bignold Middle School

WHAT IS RED?

Red is a blood-red sun
On a burning hot day,
Red will maybe be a planet,
Dry and crusty, spinning around
The outside of this world,
Close to this planet,
Red is the glowing sun,
As it settles over the houses,
Red could be an autumn tree,
In October or November,
Maybe a Red Indian
Red is a sign of danger!

Kira Hannant (8)
Bignold Middle School

ANIMAL CAR

It starts and sounds like a growling tiger,
It glides over the ground like a stalking lion,
It overtakes like a pouncing cheetah,
It slinks round corners like a prowling puma,
It stops at the lights like an animal being brought down,
The screech of tyres as it accelerates away like a howling cat,
It races someone like a bobcat running down its prey,
It reaches its destination and the engine slows to a purr
Like a tired cat after a chase it stops and drops off to sleep.

Jack Burden (11)
Bignold Middle School

LIFE OF A LEGEND

Dr No, From Russia With Love,
The first two are above.
Life as a tough secret agent,
Is not always that hard.

Girls are always after him,
But so is his boss, M,
Attention 007,
Is Q's favourite line.

Lots of Martinis, girls and guns,
Are Bond's favourite things,
No attention to the mission
And he'll get done by M.

The World Is Not Enough is new
And very popular
And it's made a bit of money,
What I just said is true!

There's another Bond film that's old,
It's made lots of money,
It was called The Spy Who Loved Me,
Bond met a nice girl called Anya.

Sean Connery was the best Bond,
Then it's Pierce Brosnan,
Roger Moore wasn't bad,
But no one can beat the best!

Lee Ivison (12)
Bignold Middle School

THE WORLD WITHIN A ROOM!

Enter
The wilderness.
Swing through the canopies,
Airy green is all around you.
Jungle!

Aengus Payne (12)
Bignold Middle School

THE DARKNESS

Darkness
Is a great god!
Pulling a silk black sheet
Over the earth and making holes
For light.

Tom David Dodsworth Lowe (12)
Bignold Middle School

GLOWING FIREFLIES

Midnight,
All is quiet.
Starfish in ocean blue . . .
Pinpricks in a piece of silk . . .
The stars.

Laura Pudney (12)
Bignold Middle School

THE NIGHT IS LIKE AN OCEAN DEEP

As night floods the sky,
starfish come out;
the rays of light spread
like tentacles -
from a jellyfish.

A shooting star
like a whale, jumping
in a large curve,
then disappearing
into the sea.

Esther Moya Read (12)
Bignold Middle School

SPRING DAYS

Flowers blooming
April showers
Baby deer,
In the sun.

Grass growing,
Daffodils, tulips,
Rabbits jumping
And having
Fun!

Becky Allen (8)
Bignold Middle School

THE NIGHT

The night is a black rat scurrying over the world,
Forever running, trying to escape from the ginger cat sun.
The moon is its sly eyes twinkling and the stars are light,
Glinting off its glossy coat.

The thunder is its heavy breathing and the lightning is it
Bearing its sharp teeth.
In the summer it's too hot to run,
So the black rat hides and the cat searches for longer.
But in the winter the cat likes to rest so the black rat
Tries to get ahead

And they continue their eternal chase, never-ending,
Never catching each other.
Maybe one day dark will be swallowed by the light.

Jack Jeffery (11)
Bignold Middle School

SUNSHINE

Sun sets over the sea,
Under the sea the fish swim happily,
Never will the fish escape
When the sun is shining so bright,
Hot is the sand, ouch,
It's burning my feet,
The sun is shining no more,
Everything's quiet, snore, snore, snore.

Samantha Landreth & Charlotte Farman (10)
Bignold Middle School

IF I WAS...

My opinion
If I was a dog I would be a sausage dog
trotting along with its posh owner in London.

If I was a flower I would be a rose
being given to a loving girl.

If I was a piece of clothing I would be a pair of baggy jeans
falling down in the city.

If I was a car I would be a Rolls Royce
cruising downtown Manhattan.

My brother's opinion
If he was a dog he would be a *big hefty* alsatian dog
patrolling viciously around its territory.

If he was a flower he would be a white rose
spreading its beautiful petals in a lovely garden.

If he was a piece of clothing he would be a track-suit bottom
all sweaty and wet after running the marathon.

If he was a car he would be a Mercedes Benz
speeding at 100mph down the motorway.

Friend's opinion
If he was a dog he would be a highland white
showing its white fur coat off in a contest.

If he was a flower he would be a daffodil
showing off its huge trumpet.

If he was a piece of clothing he would be a shoe
sprinting down a fast sports track.

If he was a car he would be a BMW
showing off its huge size and power.

Nick Smith (11)
Bignold Middle School

A VALENTINE'S DAY GIFT

Roses and flowers
A card and chocs
All wrapped up in a shiny red box
A fancy dinner
Champagne and wine
Her face comes alight
On one crystal clear night
I give her the ring,
She says 'Yes, I will'
And more joys to come still
We now have two kids
A boy and a girl
One called Lee and another called Shirl
Now we are old
We're still together
Even when we die our love'll last forever.

Martha MacLure (11)
Bignold Middle School

THE BIGNOLD ACROSTIC RAP

B ignold Middle is our school
I t has cool people (they rule!)
G oing to Bignold makes me feel cool
N othing will stop all of us rule
O ther people may think we are sad
L oads of us think they are *bad!*
D oing stuff that we all do

M akes us think we definitely rule!
I am a cross-country girl
D oing running is like running for the world
D avid Watkins is our headmaster
L oving cricket, he can't lose faster
E veryone has fun and usually there is laughter.

S afe and sound in the sun
C aring for everyone
H elpful hands guide us all the way
O ften playing every day
O ften wishing our time would come again someday
L eaving four years behind.

I t's tragic in my mind
S ometimes everyone thinks in their mind

T he best school is the one they left behind
H elping people with their work
E ven though you need to get on with your work.

B ignold is the best
E veryone thinks they can beat the best!
S ome people are not happy to leave this school
T he best is Bignold Middle School.

Carly Ivison (11)
Bignold Middle School

IF

If I was a dog I would be
a lazy spaniel sleeping all day.

If I was a flower I would be
a bright sunflower
smiling in the sun.

If I was a piece of clothing
I would be a colourful T-shirt
swinging on a washing line.

If I was a car I would be
a shining Ford Fiesta
riding on a golden beach.

Jenny Chiarotti (11)
Bignold Middle School

I GO ON A TRAIN ON PLATFORM FIVE

I go on a train on platform five
I begin to droop
I begin to sleep
I begin to snore
I wake up to ask someone 'Have we passed Diss?'
He replies 'Yes.'
The ticket man comes
He inspects my ticket
He replies: 'Sorry you've missed your stop!'
I groan.

Sophie Fox (11)
Bignold Middle School

KITE

A gust of wind blows it high into the sky.
I hold on tight,
it pulls me.
I hold on tighter.
The cord of the kite snaps,
the kite blows away.
I chase it,
but it is too fast for me.
I see it shrink as it gets
further and further and further away.
Suddenly it disappears,
gone forever.
Bye-bye kite.

James Barrett (11)
Bignold Middle School

PLAYTIME

Your chance to talk with friends,
To jump, to shout, to run,
To release that mass of energy,
A time to just have fun.

The wind is howling past the gates,
The trees, they sway and whisper,
The children button up their coats,
As the wind is getting crisper.

Pitter-patter on the roofs,
I can't believe it's rain,
Our only chance to be outdoors
And the rain has spoilt it again.

Jemila Elahcene (11)
Bignold Middle School

PLAYTIME HOURS

I was the first one out
It was quiet, all I heard was cars about
Before the door slammed
I heard tellings off
The teacher felt damned
Children coughed
It was silent
All I heard was rustling trees
And buzzing bees.

The sun is out
Clouds are all about
Children pour
From the door
The noise gradually turns up
Volume burns.

The first whistle blows
Nobody goes
It's a warning
Playtime gets boring
The second whistle goes
We are blown to the classroom
Playtime is over.

Casimir Campbell (12)
Bignold Middle School

PARENTS

Parents like you
To;
Tidy your room,
Drink your hot chocolate,
Get on with your work,
Stop daydreaming,
Not be a 'pain',
Go to acting classes,
Get up!
Go to bed at the right time,
Get them chocolate,
Make them cups of tea,
Not draw on your hand,
Wash their car,
Brush your teeth,
Be quiet when Coronation Street's on!
Turn the music down,
Go to the shop,
Hold your pen properly,
Calm down,
Not use the phone until 6 o'clock,
Be good!

Rebecca Garrod (9)
Bignold Middle School

BAD HAIR DAY

What is a bad hair day, I ask myself,
Is it when your hair goes out and doesn't return till late,
Or is it when your hair doesn't tidy its bedroom,
Just what is a bad hair day?

Felicity Daykin (10)
Bignold Middle School

PLAYTIME

A time to get rid of energy,
To make a lot of noise,
To stop the work, get out of there,
With little girls and boys.

A time to let your brain cool down,
After all that work,
Some of the children stand around,
A lot of them going berserk.

A time to listen in,
To the dinner ladies' talking,
A time to get annoyed,
By seagulls that wont stop squawking.

Constance Croot (11)
Bignold Middle School

THE VALENTINE CARD

Tell me, tell me who you are,
Love me, love me whoever you are,
Make me happy every day,
Take me out and pay, pay, pay,
Give me chocolates, flowers and sweets,
Take me out for at least a week
To Majorca, Devon or the Caribbean.
So tell me, tell me who you are,
My secret Valentine admirer.

Beth Woollsey (11)
Bignold Middle School

PARENTS

Parents like you
To;
Brush your teeth,
Fold your clothes,
Eat your lunch,
Go to bed.

Parents like you
To;
Wash your hair,
Get your breakfast,
Wear clean clothes,
Get ready for school.

Parents like you
To;
Clean your lunch box,
Run your bath,
Make your lunch,
Get good marks!

Parents like you
To;
Find their stuff,
Get their slippers,
Make the tea,
Not play on your PlayStation.

Parents like you
To;
Do lots of jobs!

Michael Warner (9)
Bignold Middle School

WHAT IS BLUE?

Blue is the waving sea
And the sky high above,
Pluto in space,
People's eyes looking around,
School sweatshirts,
Blue on the bottom of a candle,
A dolphin having its dinner,
Dripping paint!
A car you can hear,
Jeans that you wear,
A blueberry
And an alien!

Rose Edwards (8)
Bignold Middle School

PUPS ARE LIKE . . .

Pups have lots of energy
Like a motorbike after being fed.

Speeding round corners
And weaving in and out balls.

Slowing down and jumping
Into a basket like a frog
Jumping into a leaf with a splash.

Curling up to the heat of the mother
Like a caterpillar curling up to sleep.

Stephanie Clark (11)
Bignold Middle School

WHAT IS GREEN?

Leaves are shining green,
Saturn is green,
Apples are green,
Crisp and juicy,
A first-aid kit is green,
With a white cross on the top,
Brussel sprouts are green.

Danny Dyer (8)
Bignold Middle School

THE SUN

The sun is a ball of fire
It is only my desire
To see this burning flame
So high and bright in the sky
Up so high.

Jemma Seymour (12)
Bignold Middle School

MY THANK YOU LETTER

Dear Kate
Thank you for my Newcastle scarf
It is very useful for a cold and snowy day
Although I hope you don't mind
But I won't be wearing it
When I watch Arsenal play.

Shane Collier (10)
Bignold Middle School

MIDNIGHT

Nocturnal animals use this
like a tool.
It is their secret weapon.
Their pleasantness is wiped away
by hunting.
Midnight.

Badgers scrape about searching
for snails and slugs.
Rustling through leaves,
they are terrorising all
insects.
Midnight.

Hedgehogs locate slugs for
a snack.
The sight of danger shows a
small prickly ball.
A sharp case of a conker.
Prowling through the country.
Midnight.

A bush baby, lively and awake at this time.
Climbing and clinging to the tree trunk.
Her eyes large like 10 pence.
Midnight.

Gabbie Barr (9)
Colby School

MIDNIGHT

Bright stars twinkling like diamonds,
Full moon shining like a golf ball,
Bats shrieking like a thousand screams,
No sound of pure stillness.

Wind whistling
Nocturnal animals scuffling,
Cats howling on roofs like a far off screech.
A thing creeping as slowly as a leaf growing.
Trees swaying like sheaves of barley in the wind.
Noses snuffling like a mouse.
The sounds of footsteps like a drum.
Shadows growing then shrinking like a flame.

Sounds of clocks chiming like a cymbal being hit,
Eyes following you wherever you go,
A new breeze dawning,
Menacing shapes like monsters.

Jordan Curry (10)
Colby School

MIDNIGHT

Cold, silent midnight
Witching hour
Moon shines,
Owls hoot.

Cold, silent midnight
Hedgehogs scuffle,
The wind blows,
Calm, still, peaceful.

Cold, silent midnight
Leaves Rustle.
As clocks strike 12,
Morning starts night ends.

Cold, silent midnight
The start to a new day,
Darkness, blackness,
Forever there will be
Cold, silent midnight.

Joanna Cook (9)
Colby School

MIDNIGHT

Midnight, the darkest part of the lonely night,
Midnight, the lightest part of the lonely night,
As quiet as quiet can be.

Midnight, the clock strikes twelve,
People dreaming in their sleep,
Nocturnal animal searching for food.

The mist is rising, rising,
Rising, higher, higher,
Over the hills.

The night is peaceful,
Slow and calm,
With hedgehogs rustling in the leaves.

Midnight is like a flowing river,
Flowing into the dawn, people awaken,
Night is over.

Thomas Ayers (11)
Colby School

SOUNDS OF THE DARK

Sounds of the dark
Trees whistle like the gusty wind.
Fences are creaking like floorboards,
Leaves are rustling like crunching paper.

Sounds of the dark.
Wolves howling,
Dogs barking,
Cats hissing.

Sounds of the dark.
Pipes dripping like raindrops,
Plates smashing like people screaming,
Doors squeaking like mice.

Amy Watts (10)
Colby School

THE SADNESS OF JUDE

Oh her love, is like a flower
That whistles in the wind,
Her love, a free world
But now empty, like her heart.

Where is he? Why me?
She repeats in her worthy mind,
Happiness was there but now gone,
Everywhere as black as a blackbird's breast.

Nowhere to go, no one to see
Take me away, far away, somewhere new,
Does he need Jude?
Does Jude need him?

Sometimes generous, gentle even grateful man
But most of the time as wild as a wolf,
Never fair,
Still Jude's sadness will remain.

Joanna Smith (11)
Colby School

MIDNIGHT

Midnight threatens the light of day,
the moon shines on the river's bay.
The sun waits, until the moon delays
to come upon the sky.
Midnight.

Midnight rises upon the ground
only to hear the noise of hounds.
The moon sinks silently no sound,
Midnight.

Midnight is the glory of the sky.
Climbing, climbing very high
past the trees trying to get to the sky.
Glory, glory, there goes by the glooming of the sky.

Sam Evans (9)
Colby School

THE SADNESS OF JUDE

She loved a man dearly, as dearly as can be,
Until one day he let her down,
Now her happiness drowned.

When flowers blossomed like a blooming rose,
Animals grew,
All kinds of birds flew.

When people sang a happy tune,
Children played,
Corn silently swayed.

When June was as hot as a burning fire,
Branches were as bendy as wire,
Snake skin was as rubbery as a tyre.

When rabbits used to jump like kangaroos,
People used to line in a queue,
Fearsome animals locked in a zoo.

Now everything has gone
All that remains is a peaceful song.

Natasha Flowerday (10)
Colby School

MIDNIGHT

When dusk strikes,
Sun sets,
The night begins,
Shadows come out.

People sleep,
Ghosts rise with sadness in their eyes.
Small nocturnal animals awaken,
To the dark stillness of the night.

Out they come, single file,
Stern images on the horizon.
Darkness is like iron,
Cold, hard, still and grey.

Eyes glittering in the moonlight
Watch you wherever you go.
A crisp coldness has come.
The night is here,
Shadows weird.

James Katra (10)
Colby School

HAIR

Dad has short hair,
Mum has long hair,
And I've got long hair,
Together we're the hair family.

Dad has a puffer coat,
Mum has a puffer coat,
And I've got a puffer coat,
Together we're the puffer family.

Dad has a double bed,
Mum has a double bed,
And I've got a bunk bed,
Together we're the bed family.

Dad has a toy,
Mum has a toy,
And I've got lots of toys,
Together we're the toy family.

Dad has a family,
Mum has a family,
And I've got a family,
Together we're a happy family.

Hannah Dugdale (9)
George White Middle School

THE BEST FOOTBALL TEAM

Newcastle, my favourite team.
I don't know why,
I don't know when,
They all work hard to win.
They help each other
Why oh why did they lose the cup?
They are so cool.
I think they're the best.
Even if they lose
I never give up hope.
I bet in the past
They've had a better time.
They never give up hope.
I'm sure they'll get at least one cup.

James Knight (9)
Great Witchingham Primary School

MAGIC WIND

Magic wind gushing round.
So strong, pushing back and back.
So cold you feel like you're frozen.
Trees swishing side to side, some snapping in half.
Wind turning stronger and stronger.
Homes destroyed. Wind turns into gale.
Hour gone, gale turning into magic wind.
Where does the wind come from?
God sent the wind . . .
I think.

Zoe Goff (9)
Great Witchingham Primary School

RONNIE

The name is Ronnie
I invented a computer
To travel back
In time,
Dinosaur time.
I'll tell you what I saw.
Massive trees, rolling rivers.
I saw a really big dinosaur.
Bigger than two houses put together.
I was scared,
As the dinosaur approached me
I ran back in time.

Ronnie Cornell (7)
Great Witchingham Primary School

THE DOOR

Go and open the door.
Maybe there is the blazing light at night.
Go and open the door.
Perhaps there is the grey, misty morning.
Go and open the door to see the
lightness of a summer morning.
Go and open the door.
At least there'll be a draught.

Sam Robins (8)
Great Witchingham Primary School

THE DOOR

Go and open the door
Maybe there is a very fast train
Stopping at the station.

Go and open the door.
Maybe there is a daring stunt man
Getting ready to jump.
Or a big lion chasing a small rat.

Go and open the door,
Maybe there is a huge cliff
As big as a mountain.

Go and open the door.
At least there will be a draught.

Richard Harris (9)
Great Witchingham Primary School

COMPUTERS ARE FUN

Computers are like brains.
But what if all the computers in the world go wrong?
Everything will go crazy.
I would like to spend my life
On a computer, do you know?
But I need to eat, drink and sleep.

Adam Johnston (7)
Great Witchingham Primary School

ROTTEN TEETH

I eat too many sweets.
Hard and soft,
Sherbet, liquorice and chocolate.
My favourite's Twix.
I chew and crunch, suck and grind.
I bite down hard.
My teeth turn black
They need a good clean.
I brush down hard, I brush down light,
I brush around and around.
But why do I eat so many sweets?

Denise R Pead (8)
Great Witchingham Primary School

THE DOOR

Go and open the door.
Maybe there will be a magic world full of sweet things.
Go and open the door.
You might see a cowboy or an Indian fighting.
Go and open the door.
There may be a badger in your bin or a squirrel in your tree.
Go and open the door.
At least there will be a draught.

Matthew Paul (7)
Great Witchingham Primary School

A LIMERICK

A dog with a very large head,
Slept in a very big bed.
He went to school
And always played pool,
'Can I come too?' said Fred.

William Quinn (8)
Great Witchingham Primary School

CHOCOLATE

Chocolate bar in my hand
I simply have to eat you,
Quickly, very quickly.
Chocolate first
Sticky toffee and crunchy biscuit swallow.
Give me another one and another one!

Adam Sutton (8)
Great Witchingham Primary School

A LULLABY

Sleep, sleep little one
Close your eyes.
Sleep little one, sleep.
Tomorrow will bring peace and no more wars.
Sleep, sleep little one.
Maybe you will be big and strong.

Emma Long (8)
Great Witchingham Primary School

A Lullaby

Sleep, sleep little one
Tomorrow will be a new day.
Sleep, sleep little one
You will be strong.
Sleep, sleep little one.
Joy and luck will come to us.
Sleep, sleep little one.
Tomorrow, hope and peace will come.

Christopher Myhill (8)
Great Witchingham Primary School

My Annoying Little Sister

She barges in my bedroom,
She crashes at the door.
She eats with her mouth wide open,
Mashed potato swirling round,
Round and round like washing in a machine.
She won't take no for an answer
She won't ever do as I say.
But I couldn't do without her,
'Cos she's my partner today.

Faye Walker (9)
Great Witchingham Primary School

THE DOOR

Go and open the door.
There might be an alien with sharp teeth,
Or a scary werewolf waiting for you.
Go and open the door.
There might be a vampire who had eyes
which glow in the dark.
Go and open the door.
At least there will be a breeze.

Rebecca Burden (9)
Great Witchingham Primary School

THE DOOR

Go and open the door.
Maybe there is a cockerel crowing.
Maybe there is a dark dungeon,
A person screaming or a ghost.
Go and open the door.
Maybe there is a three headed dog.
Go and open the door.
At least there will be a draught.

Ella B Glendining (8)
Great Witchingham Primary School

THE DOOR

Go and open the door
perhaps you will find . . .
a beautiful bay gelding with a
shining coat.

Go and open the door
maybe you'll find . . .
a new baby laughing and
rattling its rattle.

Go and open the door
perhaps there will be
Linford Christie sprinting.

Go and open the door
maybe there will be . . .
the sound of waves rushing
up the beach.

Go and open the door
perhaps there will be . . .
all your best friends.

Rebecca Long (9)
Great Witchingham Primary School

A LIMERICK

There was a young man called Ben,
Who couldn't count up to ten.
He got up to eight
Then got in a state,
Ben just couldn't count up to ten.

Gilly Savage (7)
Great Witchingham Primary School

THE DOOR

Go and open the door.
Maybe there will be . . .
A screech of an owl in a deep forest.
The moon lighting up a dark, mysterious night.
The deep scowl of a grey and blood-stained wolf.

Go and open the door.
Perhaps there will be . . .
A rain forest with the silent beat of rain.
The silent scream of a newborn baby.

Go and open the door.
And find the . . .
Gentle cry of a seagull as it swoops across the sea.
The words of a story being read to a child
fade away into the night.

Go and open the door.

At least there'll be a draught.

Vita Sunter (8)
Great Witchingham Primary School

A LULLABY

Sleep, sleep little one, close your eyes.
Sleep little one.
Sleep, tomorrow you will get a new teddy bear and you can play with it.
Sleep, tomorrow the postman will come in his van with a letter.
Sleep, tomorrow the birds will sing in the trees.
Sleep, tomorrow there might be sunshine coming through the trees.

Katie Symonds (9)
Great Witchingham Primary School

Do Not Smoke

Do not smoke,
It's bad for your health,
You lose all your money,
And all your wealth.

Do not smoke,
Just think how upset,
All your family,
And friends will get.

Do not smoke,
Give up while there's time,
Thousands are dying,
While you read this rhyme.

Kieron Bacon (9)
Marsham Primary School

Dyslexic

My spelling's bad,
My writing's worse,
English lessons,
Are a curse,
My teacher she has tested me
She says that I am bright,
But when I write my work down,
It never comes out right.
Children say I'm stupid,
Others say I'm thick,
But teacher knows the reason why,
I am a dyslexic.

Tristan Bacon (10)
Marsham Primary School

THE UNICORN

A pure white horse
With a silver horn
Is a mystical beast
Called a unicorn
He is a magic horse
Not everyone can see
Unless you've imagination
Just like me.

Ashley Bacon (9)
Marsham Primary School

A POPPY

A poppy is red
A poppy is green
A poppy is beautiful
A poppy is about the war
A poppy is for a life.

Thomas Medler (8)
Marsham Primary School

MY RABBIT

Rabbit,
He is fluffy,
My rabbit is called Tom,
He lives in his warm, cosy hutch,
Love him.

Lisa Halls (9)
Marsham Primary School

DRAGONS

When I went to bed last night,
I dreamt I was a dragon,
Who flew up high
Who roared out fire
Who was scaly,
Green and silver.
How nice I was,
How beautiful I looked.
But then it ended.
I woke up and . . .
Surprise! I found I was a dragon.
Who rode through the sky
I was scaly, purple and green
With sharp, shiny teeth and
Glowing, red eyes.
I leapt and swooped down,
Then landed in a sparkling place
With gold and silver on the wall,
A sign, said 'Beware, Beware.'

Jenny Michell Revell (9)
Mulbarton Middle School

PARENTS

Parents, bossy, rude and spiteful.
What else can you get?
Mum, bossy, spiteful and kind less.
Dad, bossy, rude, spiteful and mindless.

Parents, let brother or sister off, nearly always blame you
What else are they?
Mindless, kind less,
Rude, always in a mood.

Parents, 'Feed the rabbits, clean the fish out.'
Horrible aren't they?
They moan
And they groan.

Parents. Wish they were dead?
No way!
I like my parents just the way they are!
Well sometimes!

Sarah Wyatt (8)
Mulbarton Middle School

MY DOG

My dog has sharp teeth
She can bite through
Your jumper or
She might bite you instead.

My dog can run fast
And when she sees a duck
She will run after it.

My dog is wild
Because she always gets vicious
When she sees my dad.

My dog does not live outside
She lives in a basket
She loves her basket.

My dogs has lots of treats
She goes into the field
And has a walk.

James Stickland (8)
Mulbarton Middle School

SCHOOL INSPECTORS

Now stop fiddling with that chewing gum.
Melanie don't stick it up your bum!
The school inspector's going to come!
Abby please stop sucking your thumb.
Jenna stop calling Ben dumb.

Hayley do stop entertaining.
While your teacher is explaining.

Thomas I'm trying to talk to you.
James! Stop sending love letters to . . . !
Lawrence please stop shouting 'Mooo!'
Get away from my desk. Just shoo!
Michelle stop dancing on the table. Please do.

Laura why did you push Brian to the ground?
Carl please will you stop clowning around.
Look, don't even make a sound.
'Miss Burgess, please stop shouting to your class'
Oh is Miss Burgess going to pass?
'You're fired!'

Claire Ashby (8)
Mulbarton Middle School

I WANT TO BE A CRAWLING CATERPILLAR

I want to be a crawling caterpillar,
I'll be crawling on your vegetables, vegetables,
Yummy, yum, yum
I'll be crawling on your vegetables
All day long.

Duncan Lloyd Baker (8)
Mulbarton Middle School

My World

My world would be,
Where chocolate would grow on every tree.
Lemonade would fill the pond,
I would drink it whilst watching James Bond,
In the corner, a money bush,
There was a jam ball so I gave it a push,
It rolled over a sherbet patch,
And into the pond with a splash,
I love the chocolate flowers,
I slipped over and found a jam triangle,
Oh! dear my head is full of sweets
I can't remember them all
So I'll have to finish this poem with
Goodbye to one and all.

Sarah Mayhew (8)
Mulbarton Middle School

I WISH!

I wish I could be a footballer when I grow up.
I wish we could have more playtime.
I hope I will live to 150.
I wish I become famous when I grow up.
We all hope Earth still lives.
I wish we had more land like Russia!

I wish!

Matthew Newson (8)
Mulbarton Middle School

MONKEYS!

Monkeys swing about a cage,
Even if they're adult age.
Gorillas are always messing about
But their mum's don't shout
'Stop being a monkey!'

Apes are supposed to have a lot of brains
But they just swing around and play games!
But what if they went to school
No, the teachers are not that cool!
But if they did it wouldn't be fair,
They don't get any homework!

Hey, next time my mum calls me a monkey
I'll say 'I'd quite like to be a monkey for . . .
They don't have to go to school.'
Which would be very cool!
They don't get any homework
They can always play the fool.
I think being a monkey
Would be cool!
Yeah I agree with mum
Now I'm a monkey
I can start to have fun!

Abby Kirk (9)
Mulbarton Middle School

WHEN I WAS YOUNG

When I was 1 I could count to three
When I was 2 I could climb a tree
When I was 3 I could eat a cookie
When I was 4 I could boogie
When I was 5 I liked bee hives
When I was 6 I was alive
When I was 7 I fancied Kevin
When I was 8 I went to Heaven
When I was 9 I could build a den
Now I am 10 and I've got a boyfriend.

Jay Baker (9)
Mulbarton Middle School

HAPPINESS

Happiness is kindness
Happiness is love
Happiness is caring
Happiness is the sun
Happiness is when the stars twinkle
Happiness is the moon
Happiness is to be happy.

Happiness!

Jenna Clarke-Frary (8)
Mulbarton Middle School

PARADISE ISLAND

My paradise island is a land of peace
With a big relaxing beach
I would sit near the sherbet lake
Listening to a cake bake.
Lots of wildlife come to me
Leading was a giant bee.
The beautiful unicorn dancing around.
He said 'I could buy his ball for a pound.'
So I took it home
It's still there now,
And it will remind me of my paradise island.

Kirsty Barrett (9)
Mulbarton Middle School

HANDS

Hands can be good, hands can be bad
Hands can be sensible, hands can be mad
Hands can pick noses, hands can pinch bums
Hands can plant gardens, hands can help work out sums
Hands can make people happy, hands can make people sad
Hands can be good, hands can be bad!

Jenny Bradley (8)
Mulbarton Middle School

I Love My Mum

Because my mum loves me
Because my mum is nice to me
Because my mum is nice to Ashley my big brother.

I love my mum
Because she plays with me
Because mum helps me
I love my mum lots!

Lawrence Burton (8)
Mulbarton Middle School

Earth

Earth is dying
Because of us
What did animals do to the Earth?
Nothing!
We did it
Think about it. Think about it . . .

Brian Mills (8)
Mulbarton Middle School

Say 'Goodbye' To The FA Cup

I wish, I wish,
We'd win the FA Cup.
Oh! how I do wish
Fulham would win the FA Cup!

Dreams just don't come true!
Oh boo hoo hoo.

Out of it already?
Tottenham, City, Wimbledon and Leicester!
What more can you get?

Tottenham 3-1, Wimbledon 3-0
Norwich City 4-0 and 2-0
Up at Leicester then lose
How bad is it?

Manchester United won't win it,
Liverpool FC, ain't got a chance,
So who will win it in 2000?
Goodbye to Wembley
Goodbye to the FA Cup
Me money's on Leicester!
Unfortunately!

Ben Shearing (8)
Mulbarton Middle School

THE SUNSET

The sun was setting in the sky
Like a fire that's just been lit.
But when the sun is fully set
The fire has been put out
But when the sun gets up
The fire is being burnt.

Pip Morgan (8)
Mulbarton Middle School

GAMES

Games are good
Football, netball
All over!
The games are good
Because I like playing them
So do other people.
I like games!

Sam Catton (8)
Mulbarton Middle School

UP IN THE SKY

In the sky
Floating around
A mile from the ground
I'm going to Africa
In a hot air balloon . . .
Up, up and away!

Morgan Williams (9)
Mulbarton Middle School

BONFIRE NIGHT

Fireworks crackle in the sky
See the rockets how they fly
The bonfire brightens up the night
Loud bangs give small children a fright

Catherine wheels and Roman candles
Pretty to watch but dangerous to handle
Light the fuse and stand well back
Gasp in delight as they whistle and crack

Spinning, shooting, whirling, whizzing
The fireworks look just like they're fizzing
Pops and bangs and coloured flashes
Then all that's left are bonfire ashes.

Nathan Goose (10)
Notre Dame Prep School

I WISH I COULD FLY!

I wish I could fly,
Right up in the sky,
Dancing and prancing,
Within the clouds,
Their shapes are wonderful,
Big dragons, elephants and little angels.

I lie in bed fast asleep,
And dream of floating on clouds,
With angels standing by,
Up, up, up,
I really wish I could fly!

Emma Lusher (9)
Notre Dame Prep School

WHY?

Last week my mum was really ill,
She got worse and worse,
She had to go to the hospital
We went to see the nurse.

The nurse came to me and said
'You have to be strong and bold
You see your mother is dead
She died from a really bad cold.'

Why is it my mother?
Why did she have to go?
There's so many answers to questions
That I really want to know!

Amy Holmwood (10)
Notre Dame Prep School

MY MUM

When I'm sad and lonely,
When I'm feeling alone,
When I feel there is no one left
I'll always have one special friend
Who will always be there forever more,
She's always near,
When I shed a tear
She's my special friend.
That's Mum.

Meike Eliza Yallop (10)
Notre Dame Prep School

THE WILD HOUSE

In through the door
And up the stairs
Into the first bedroom known as Claire's.
Bright red walls
And posters on the door
Toys on the table and homework on the floor.

On to the next room whose could it be?
Walk in. Let's see
Green and orange striped walls
And in the corner footballs
This room belongs to James
He likes to make a mess and play different games.

And poor me for I'm the cleaner
You couldn't get a job any meaner
Hoover, tidy look after James and Claire
And everyone knows that they're a right pair!

Madelaine Coutinho (9)
Notre Dame Prep School

THE WOOD

The squirrels jumping gaily around,
Collecting red berries from the ground.
A green woodpecker making a home,
The badger making its way to a set.

Two rabbits hopping away,
A sly, crafty fox padding behind!
A damp toad splashing around,
In the sparkling stream.

The big bright sun,
Shining through the dusty trees.
A cooing dove making a nest,
In a great beech tree.

As I walk to the edge of the wood,
I turn back and look at what I passed.
The woodpecker still pecking away,
It is now sunset, what a beautiful view!

Bryony Stanley (9)
Notre Dame Prep School

SEASONS

Autumn days when the grass is frosted.
Chestnuts falling from the trees.
Wearing hats, scarves and gloves to keep
The cold from frosting me.

Winter days when the snow is falling
December mornings when the car won't start.
January days when the lake is frozen.
February rains make huge floods.

Spring cold mornings new bulbs blooming.
Baby animals come to life.
Days grow longer
Nights grow shorter.

Summer days we're off to the beach
Swimming in the English sea
Summer holidays across the Channel
And then all of a sudden we're in autumn again.

Zoë Tipler (10)
Notre Dame Prep School

MONDAYS, TUESDAYS, HAPPY DAYS

On the first day of May
We were sitting in the sun,
Rushing all our homework,
To have a lot of fun.

Dad got out the mower and
Mum put on her shorts,
We all got out our racquets,
For the tennis courts.

Our friends came round to play
With us so we were really glad
So we didn't have to pester
Poor old Mum and Dad.

We put on our helmets and
Jumped on our bikes, 'Hoorah,'
And rushed off to the play park,
With all our friends to play.

Running up the jungle walk
Going down the slide,
Many things to play on,
Not paying for a ride.

Laura Sheppeck (11)
Notre Dame Prep School

SCHOOL

You learn at school maths, division, history.
All the teachers are kind, give you homework every night.
The next day another day of school
Oh! Look I got a house point.

Noise everywhere kids running down the corridor.
Hear the chalk scraping against the blackboard.
All the people at the lunch table making noise.
Fire bells going off.

Matthew Adlard (8)
Notre Dame Prep School

IT'S ALWAYS ME

You always blame me
Like yesterday the sun was shining
And as usual you blamed it on me.
I did not spill the water.
I did not eat all the sweets.
It was Toby I know it was.
I even saw him do it.
Then on Monday when the workmen came
To paint a wall,
My friend Jenny spilt the paint.
She blamed it on me,
Now I've had enough.
I'm going to Mum and Dad
To try and sort it out.
I'm going to be brave
Like a man
Or I could just wait
Until Mum and Dad find out
That it really wasn't me.
Yes I think that's best.

Roxanne Mitchell (10)
Notre Dame Prep School

2000

Come and celebrate!
2000 is here!
Fireworks and lights
What a delight!

The special year is here!
Exciting for youngsters
Jesus is 2000 today
Jesus was born two thousand years ago.

Massive parties full of fun
Try and party till the rise of the sun!
Lots of food and drinks
A lot of people to celebrate the year
2000 millennium party!

Katrina Chia (8)
Notre Dame Prep School

AN OWL'S NATURE

An owl flying through the air,
With the night wind blowing cold and chilly.
Stooping with no sound,
Swiftly moves down to the ground.
Sneaking to catch its prey
Rats running to get away.
After the owl's had a bite,
He sleeps in a tree for the night.

Nicola Shattock (10)
Notre Dame Prep School

THE INDIAN CAMPFIRE SONG

We fight with bones and sticks
And we collect quibix
Pow, wow, pow, wow
We're the men of the black and brown cow, how.
All of us are red men
Feathers in our hair men
Down among the dead men, yeuch
Pow, wow, pow, wow, pow, wow.

When we die we go to heaven
To protect God from Satan
Pow, wow, pow, wow
We're the men of the black and brown cow, how
All of us are red men
Feathers in our hair men
Down among the dead men, yeuch
Pow, wow, pow, wow, pow, wow.

Joseph Malpas (8)
Notre Dame Prep School

THE JUNGLE

The shiny green leaves that sparkle in the sun
The gold leaves, monkeys everywhere
Trees which almost touch the sun
Cheetahs prancing and dancing
Elephants eating from the wet ground
The jungle is really busy when you explore.

Joshua Pond (9)
Notre Dame Prep School

WATERFALLS

Waterfalls big ones, small ones.
Swishing to and fro.
Going down
Faster faster,
Then suddenly splash!

Waterfalls
Are fascinating things
Cascading
Spraying water everywhere
Deafening water
Rippling rapids
Rushing down the cliff.

Megan Groen (9)
Notre Dame Prep School

INSIDE THE MANDRILL'S BITE

Inside the mandrill's bite a river
Inside the river the mandrill's teeth
Inside the mandrill's teeth the trees
Inside the trees the mandrill's fur
Inside the mandrill's fur a forest
Inside the forest the mandrill's feet
Inside the mandrill's feet a vine
Inside the mandrill's mouth the cry of a tiger
Inside the cry of a tiger the mandrill's eyes.

Samuel Tawn (9)
Notre Dame Prep School

CIGAR

Cigar
Smoke
Twirling
Into the air
With a mark
Strasbourg
1892
Awful smells
People
Wheezing
Addicted
Yuk!

James Brown (9)
Notre Dame Prep School

A PLANE

Quicker than lightning, quicker than a splash,
Swimming pools and houses, factories by in a flash,
Zooming along like a hungry lion,
Straight across the city, cars and a siren.
All of the sights of the green, green grass,
Swiftly swooping, now it's past;
And over and over, in the wink of an eye,
Seas of green trees swishing by.

Anandi Green (9)
Notre Dame Prep School

WILL SANTA EVER COME?

I've been waiting for ages
Will he ever come?
Will who ever come?
Santa, silly, are you dumb?

I've been waiting for ages
I know he will come
But when, I ask you?
When will he come?

It's Christmas Eve at last
Now he will come
To bring me toys
He's been at *last!*

Florence John (8)
Notre Dame Prep School

FRIES

They're straight and salty,
Crunchy and malty.
Whenever you eat them they crunch!
When you put on vinegar
They give you a fright,
They dry out your mouth
And make your nose tickle.
That's what I like about fries!

Jimmy Wheeler (10)
Notre Dame Prep School

My Robot

I made a robot a few weeks ago
I like to call him Wheels,
I've taught him to do all kinds of tricks
And told him never to steal.

He tidies my room, plays hide-and-seek
There's funny places where he hides,
He plays with the cat, washes the dishes
And we read each other's minds.

But two days ago my brother found out
He broke it and chucked it outside,
So I tried to get out to rescue him
But my brother wasn't on my side.

'No, no, no! Get back to your room
Or I'll tell Mum and Dad.'
I looked out the window
And felt extremely sad.

The next morning I ran outside
Found him and grabbed him by arm,
I took him to my room
And started to repair him.

So now I'm connecting his leg joint on
He's ever so nearly done,
I'm going to add a few things on
Oh! This will be fun!

Michael Saunders (10)
Notre Dame Prep School

THE NIGHT

The night is black and gloomy
The owl is swooping around the sky
The moon is shining in the sky
In the dark dark night.

The cats are mewing at night
The dogs are barking
Mice are scurrying along the path
The owl is singing too-wit-too-woo.

The stars are shining in the sky
The moon is shining in the night
Sometimes you see the North star
In the dark night

When I sleep I can hear my cat playing
My light comes on outside at night
The trees are glowing in the dark dark night
I love the night.

Rebecca Thouless (9)
Notre Dame Prep School

NIGHT

Cats come out at night,
Cats sometimes fight,
Cats climb trees,
Black, black trees.

The moon shines bright,
Very, very bright,
Brighter than a torch,
Bright as the stars.

Owls come out at night,
Hooting keeping awake,
Gliding without a sound,
Hunting mice and rats.

Hundreds and hundreds of stars,
Twinkling stars
Shooting stars
Bright stars.

Georgia Levell (9)
Notre Dame Prep School

UNDER THE COVERS

Under the covers
What do you see?
A teddy with one eye
A doll with one arm
My hot water bottle so warm.

Under the covers
What do you see?
My pillow
A toy beanie from McDonald's
A book from school oh dear oh dear.

Under the covers
What do you see?
A cuddly bee
Just for me
A pizza from last night's dinner
A book of the Earth I read last night.

Bethany Richards (8)
Notre Dame Prep School

CHRISTMASTIME

I love Christmastime
When Santa comes
But when will he come, is the thing
He is quite a snoozer!

Lights outside
So I can't get to sleep
But they look so nice
Can't they turn them off though.

It's snowing outside
Which adds to the fun
It's making a Christmas scene for
Christmas day!

Lisa Carroll (9)
Notre Dame Prep School

THE WEEKEND!

Busy, busy school days we've got a rest at last,
Playing games, watching TV, it is such a blast.
Mum and Dad don't nag me to get out of my bed,
We could sleep forever, but we'd rather play instead.
Homework still needs doing, we don't get off that light,
But at least we have a choice to do it day or night!
My favourite things to do each day, change every minute,
Biking, walking, reading, the park, there is nothing to it.
But now it's Monday afternoon this week's over at an end
So spare a thought for me right now, your happy, rested friend.

Jenny Sheppeck (11)
Notre Dame Prep School

IMAGINE IF . . .

Imagine if frogs couldn't hop,
And dogs could shop!
Imagine if couches could talk,
And, imagine if adults couldn't walk.

Imagine if there were green cats,
And yellow bats.
Imagine money could grow on trees,
And, imagine if there are such things as blue leaves.

Imagine if cartoons were real,
And, an orange you couldn't peel.
Imagine if birds couldn't fly,
And if children didn't lie!

Ben Meen (8)
Notre Dame Prep School

HAMSTERS

Hamsters are wonderful pets,
They are nocturnal and greedy,
I have a hamster called Monty,
He is sweet and cuddly,
And likes to run in his wheel.

He has to be cleaned out once a week,
And I put some fresh sawdust in his cage,
He likes to be handled a lot,
Although he sometimes bites,
And tries to run away.

Camilla Brake (10)
Notre Dame Prep School

CHRISTMAS POEM

On the table lots of things
Turkey wishes everything
Parcels presents for everyone
Hope you all have lots of fun.

Christmas tree in the lounge
Lights and baubles all around
I put the angel on the tree
And everyone stares up at me.

Father Christmas on his way
With lots of toys on his sleigh
Everyone knows it's Christmas Day
Please can we go out to play?

Rosie Black (8)
Notre Dame Prep School

FRIENDS

Friends can be helpful,
They can really care,
They never ever hurt you,
Or pull your hair.

They talk to you at night
And play with you all day,
They never leave you out
And they never walk away.

They give you lots of comfort,
When you're feeling sad.
Sometimes they are serious,
Sometimes they're really mad!

They help you with your work
Which you haven't done,
So all in all,
Friends are lots of fun!

Eloise Petzold (11)
Notre Dame Prep School

SOUP

Empty tums find soup useful,
Babies love it by the spoonful,
Tomato, leek and spicy bean,
Carrot, red pepper, chicken and cream.

Stir the soup into the pot,
Heat it till it's flaming hot.
Add a herb, mix in a spice,
Till it tastes really nice.

Mix it until it's really thick,
Pick up the spoon and give it a lick,
It's five o'clock time to be fed,
Get out the soup, get out the bread!

Susannah Ramjeet (11)
Notre Dame Prep School

THE CONGO BONGO

It's one hot summer
In the middle of the jungle
Here comes the funky monkey
Advertising 'Congo Bongo!'

It's the coolest club
Since the 'Animalia Ball'
It's fifty foot square
And twenty foot tall.

Here come the elephants
Singing their song
And now ladies and gentlemen
At forty foot it's *King Kong!*

The famous Tina Tiger
Is singing 'Jungle Rumblebeat'
Look, there's the dancing hippo
What a *big* treat!

The great fat armadillo
Is never gonna stop
He's the fool up in the pool
Doing the big belly flop

You see Prince Lion flirting
With every lioness
Especially the one that
Wears the pink and purple dress

This is the kind of party
For every beast and cub
And if you really want to come
It's called the *Congo Bongo Club.*

Oliver Mortham (11)
Notre Dame Prep School

MY DREAM VALENTINE

I have a dream valentine
He's tall, handsome and fair,
My mother said there is no chance
For those kind of men are rare.

I want a man with a hairy chest
So I can rest my head,
A man with soft hands and a heart
I'd like it if he were called Ted.

I'd like to pretend he was my teddy bear
So I could cuddle up to him at night,
And in the morning when he has his shower
His hair would be like golden light.

He'd be a guy who's trendy
And does the popstar groove,
All the girls would go for him
You should watch his dancing moves.

The twists and twirls will amaze you
He'll go flying in the air,
His singing is like Boyzone
The girls are screaming there.

He would take me to a romantic restaurant
And we'd sit in candle light,
We would go to a disco
And dance and party all night.

But now my dream is over
Night's gone and morning's just the same,
But tomorrow night
I can dream my dream all over again.

Hannah Donaldson-Davidson (11)
Notre Dame Prep School

THE SNOW POEM

The snow has started to fall
All trees stand firm and tall
They are all smothered in a blanket of snow
The chilling winter wind has started to blow

The snow isn't making a single sound
It is covering all the ground
The robin is heading for his nest
But even through the thick snow you can see his red breast

I slide down the hill in my sleigh
Snowball fights are fun to play
I am very cold although
I really do love the snow.

Joshua Middleton (11)
Notre Dame Prep School

WHEN I GROW UP I WANT TO BE . . .

When I grow up I want to be
A company accountant.
Multiplication, division, addition and subtraction.
A six figure salary would give me satisfaction.

When I grow up I want to be
A big tennis pro.
Game, set, match and champion,
I'd beat that brilliant Tim Henman.

When I grow up I want to be
A famous astronaut.
Countdown, lift off, orbit and moon base,
I'd go down in history in the scientific race.

When I grow up I want to be
A solicitor in court.
Judge, jury, wig and gown,
I'd serve people, queen and crown.

Bethany Flatt (10)
Notre Dame Prep School

A PIECE OF ART

A piece of art
To pin on the wall,
My own DIY
I am hopeless of course.
A nail, my thumb.
A plaster ready
Let my painted boat
Sail my room on an ocean,
Of green and blue.
The shelves are next.
A tin of red paint
The large drill too.
A screw in the wall
And a hammer on the floor
Whatever next?

Rachel Holden (11)
Notre Dame Prep School

RIVER SNAKE

The river snake glistens in the
        sun
For the river snake's journey has
        just begun
It's going to topple over
        the edge
And sink its venom into
        the riverbed
The river snake sheds its skin
        on the rocks
It travels on and never
        stops
The river snake tires but it
        never shows
It travels along waterfalls
        you know.

Catherine Cutts (10)
Reepham Primary School

HAUNTED

H aunted house creepy and horrifying
A nd the ghosts are terrifying
U nder the stairs it is dusty
N ever walk in the bedroom it tastes musty
T he stairs are creaky
E lectric cables are alive and creepy
D amp demons are coming out, be scared out and about.

Laura Jarvis (10)
Reepham Primary School

GLIMMERING WATERFALL

The coldness of the water,
It's hitting my boiling limbs,
The sun's beam on the waterfall,
Is like a distant light.

As it gushes down the stream,
It glistens in the sunlight,
As it reaches the end of the stream,
There is a river full of mist.

The bank is damp and
It glistens in the sunlight,
And it smells of fish.
As the waves flow down the stream,
It hits a foamy bank.

Jade Hardesty (9)
Reepham Primary School

WATERFALL

Creeping down the quiet stream,
     Steady all the way.
    Suddenly I start to feel a sudden drop,
      Bouncing off the falling rocks
         Feeling very unsafe,
       Pouncing down to a rippling splash.
             Fish all around me,
              Maybe it was the end?
             Maybe it had just begun?

Lizzy Carey (9)
Reepham Primary School

WATERFALL WONDERS

The waterfall bubbling and spitting,
As it hits the frothing plunge pool.
It goes under like a diver,
The rough current from the flow firmly topples off.
> Crashing splashing splosh.

The water flowing down the stream,
Quickly sparkles as it goes.
Hear the fizzing round the bend,
As it trickles down again.
> Crashing splashing splosh.

Suddenly the water hits the sea,
As it says goodbye to me.
I lose it as it goes far out,
Wait I hear myself shout.
I never see it again,
> Crashing splashing splosh.

Rachel Stringer (9)
Reepham Primary School

WATERFALL

Rushing and gushing like a hungry cheetah,
Creeping like a stalking cat.
Pouncing down to a splash,
Chasing the smell of the fresh sea air.
Ripping at the rocks trying to catch its prey.

James Harden (10)
Reepham Primary School

SPLISH, SPLASH

Splish, splash, splish, splosh
The water's falling down.
Splish, splosh, splish, splosh,
Trying not to make a sound.

A waterfall's a living thing,
Just like you and me.
Especially in my dreams,
It will have arms and legs and
Will speak to me.

Splish, splash, splish, splosh,
The water's falling down.
Splish, splosh, splish, splosh,
Trying not to make a sound.

Danielle Laye (9)
Reepham Primary School

HAUNTED

H   orrifying ghosts and creepy ghouls,
A   ll in the bedroom looking like fools.
U   nder the stairs are piles of demons,
N   ever to have any good feelings.
T   errifying bats up in the attic,
E   merge from their hiding places when people panic
D   eceiving locks on this old house, dare anyone buy it
        they might get . . . *spooked out!*

Theo Gadalla (10)
Reepham Primary School

WHAT CAN YOU SEE?

What can you see in the waterfall
         that isn't really there?
Well I can see a big scary grizzly bear!

What can you see in the waterfall
         that isn't really there?
Well I can see a most beautiful and
         lovely white deer!

What can you see in the waterfall
         that isn't really there?
Well I can see a wonderful little
         baby brown hare!

What can you see in the waterfall
         that isn't really there?
Well I can see a scrumptious big
         pint of beer!

Daisy Hood (10)
Reepham Primary School

SPRING

New buds on trees,
Tulips and daffodils underneath.
In the shadows.
Children playing in the sun.
Woods covered in bluebells.
Birds singing in the woodland.

Matthew Saunders (11)
Reepham Primary School

SPELL OF THE MILLENNIUM

So as not to be a bore;
Chuck in the N64,
With more ingredients in the air
Fling in the bubble chair
Millennium Bug is around the corner,
Right next door to Ray's sauna,
Round and round the washing machine,
Making ingredients more than clean,
Racing through the Ariel powder,
Beginning to get even cloudier,
With Jack Ryder, so hunky
Chuck in a sea monkey,
Just to make you feel at home,
Toss in the Millennium Dome,
Millennium Bug is around the corner,
Right next door to Ray's sauna,
Round and round the washing machine,
Making ingredients more than clean,
Racing through the Ariel powder,
Beginning to get even cloudier.
Cut it up piece by piece,
Throw in the Lotus Elise.
Grind up the CDs
Millennium Bug is around the corner,
Right next door to Ray's sauna,
Round and round the washing machine,
Making ingredients more than clean,
Racing through the Ariel powder,
Beginning to get even cloudier,
Zoe Ball and Norman Cook,
Have got married, what a look,
Giving each other lots of hugs,
Better watch out for the Millennium Bug!

Sarah Warren (11)
Reepham Primary School

WATERFALL!

Trickle trickle down comes
The glistening water,
Flows over the rocks,
Down comes the water.

Fresh clean summery smell,
Not like smelly socks,
Down comes the water.

It flows down the stream,
Like flowing into a dream,
Down comes the water.

As it hits the ground,
It makes a big sound,
Down comes the water.

Crash as it hits the bottom,
It makes lots of bubbles,
But it doesn't make many puddles,
Down comes the water.

Sophie Watterson (10)
Reepham Primary School

WINTER

Icicles hanging from the buildings,
Frost on the ground.
Howling blizzards,
Slippery ice on the roads.
Snowmen are made.

And melting.
Gloomy nights,
Wind blowing fiercely.
Fog on the roads.
Drivers cannot see.
Winter is here.

Robert Jones (10)
Reepham Primary School

THE SOLAR SYSTEM

T   he solar system full of planets,
H   uge, part of a massive galaxy.
E   very star possibly having its own little solar system.

S   tars everywhere, the sun being our own,
O   ur solar system, one of many.
L   ight years away someone, something
     will be doing the same as me,
A   cross the universe people have dreamed of travelling,
R   acing through the stars people will one day do.

S   pace is all around us, everywhere we go,
     everything we see is in space,
Y   ears have passed since the last man on the moon,
S   pace shuttles are being built, so are space stations,
T   ime will pass and there will be space hotels,
E   veryone will one day travel in space, it will
     become cheap, available to all,
M   illions of years ago the solar system was made,
     in millions of years' time, it will be destroyed.

James Dixon (10)
Reepham Primary School

WINTER

Winter blowing.
Stars twinkling.
Gloomy night;
Gloomy day.
Chilly night,
Chilly day!
Grass blowing,
Snowmen building.
No sound.
All ice and snow.
Animals hibernating.
Winter!

Martin Secker (10)
Reepham Primary School

HAUNTED!

H aunted houses dark and creaky,
A ll cobwebby dull, misty and creepy.
U nder the floorboards cold and gloomy,
N ow where it is all scary and spooky.
T he haunted house as it is now called,
E ndless howls from the ghost and ghouls.
D angerous dungeons all musty and rusty,
    I open the door and
                    Ahhh!

Amy Bowden (10)
Reepham Primary School

THE WATERFALL

What is a waterfall?
It's a sheet of glass,
In a pane of rock.

What is a waterfall?
It's a bright blue snake,
Slithering through the grass.

What is a waterfall?
It's an invisible cauldron,
Bubbling over at the bottom.

What is a waterfall?
It's an imaginary man,
Always moving never stopping.

What is a waterfall?

Alex McArthur (10)
Reepham Primary School

WINTER

Children in winter,
Playing outside in the snow,
Making snowmen
Very cold!
Snow drops
Tip tap on the roof.
The snow hanging on the wall.
It's winter!

Ricky Shaw (9)
Reepham Primary School

CAN YOU SEE?

Can you see that face in the waterfall?
No, but I can hear a faint call from the waterfall,
Can you hear the faint call from the waterfall?
No, but I can feel the hard breathing of the waterfall,
Can you feel the hard breathing of the waterfall?
No, but I can taste the saliva from the waterfall.

Can you taste the saliva from the waterfall?
No, I can only taste the waterfall.
Can you feel the hard breathing of the waterfall?
No, I can only feel the waterfall.
Can you hear the faint call from the waterfall?
No, I can only hear the waterfall.
Can you see that face in the waterfall?
No, I can only see the waterfall.

But surely you can see something?
I can see something, but only in my head.

Stuart Gates (10)
Reepham Primary School

HAUNTED HOUSE

H allowe'en
A ll the time in the castle
U nder the tombstones
N ight-time. I see those terrible things
T rees blowing
E vil screams echo
D reaming and dreaming all the time.

Robert Jones (10)
Reepham Primary School

A MILLENNIUM PRAYER

When I grow up I hope the world
Will be colourful and clean.
The lovely scenic earth will stay with us.
The fields remain true green.

I hope the world will help others in need
And wars will not be seen
And people won't pollute the seas
And poor kids will be clean.

I wish the rich shared with the poor,
And we celebrated our colour.
But most of all, I pray Dear Lord,
We care for one another.

Stacey High (9)
Reepham Primary School

SPRING

When spring is here
Everybody will cheer!
Children in the sun,
Having lots of fun.
Bees buzzing in the air,
They are flying everywhere.
The wind gently blowing,
New leaves are growing.

Shane Brock (9)
Reepham Primary School

I WONDER

What does the future hold?
Will armies fight battles
And will they not eat cattle?
I wonder, I wonder, I wonder . . .

Will trees fall dead from the sky
And in the battles people die?
When the spring comes, will people stare?
I wonder, I wonder, I wonder . . .

Will animals scatter through the hills?
Will people not pay bills?
I don't know what the future will hold
I wonder, I wonder, I wonder . . .

Ian Gibbons (8)
Reepham Primary School

SPRINGTIME

Bees buzzing in their nest,
People cheering in the crowds.
Daffodils glowing in the sun,
Children playing in the wind.
Leaves scattering,
Birds singing in the trees.
Ice-cream van chugging up the hill.
Gently petals drop,
Spring.

Adam Meek & Andrew Hooker (9)
Reepham Primary School

MILLENNIUM SPELL

Bubble chair goes into a flare
Washing machine spins in like a dream
Toss in plane and a Virgin train.
Throw in a sea cat and a baseball bat.

Millennium Dome, Millennium Dome, Modern Gnome
Wish and throw

Add a PC and a DVD.
Throw in a Sega Dreamcast, it will go off with a blast
Plus stealth bombers and American dollars.

Millennium Dome, Millennium Dome, Modern Gnone
Wish and throw

Mix a chopper and a helicopter, burn with a flamethrower
Mince with a lawnmower.

Millennium Dome, Millennium Dome, Modern Gnome
Wish and throw.

David Hilton (10)
Reepham Primary School

HAUNTED

H   allowe'en a terrible sight
A   aahhh shout the shrill frightened voices
U   nder the tombstones bubble and hiss
N   ever again except, All Hallows Eve!
T   oads and frogs - beetly bugs
E   vil ghosts, hags and horrors
D   eep in darkness, sun comes no more.

Daniel Fromings (9)
Reepham Primary School

EVER-ENDING TIGERS

They're dying out
Never coming back
Will they live?
Will they still move about?

They're shot
Trapped
The tigers I mean
It's man killing the lot

I've got an idea how to save them
Stop the men
But they say 'No'
We've got to blame them

Guns must stop
For they're being shot
Give them one chance
It's all they need . . .
. . . Please . . . Please

'No' the men roar
The cubs that roam
Please go home
For the territory
For the trees they gnaw

Hiding safe home in the den
From men trapping them
Guns won't end
It's not safe
Don't go out again

End with a sleep
Don't wake!
Can't wake!
Or disturb . . .
Neither look up
Or peep.

For this isn't asleep
This is the end.

Hannah Shaw (9)
Reepham Primary School

HAUNTED HOUSE

H orrific house, around the ghosts do creep.
A round and about the walls, the zombies so deep.
U nder the floorboards corpses rot,
N o one will visit them or they may be boiled in a pot
T aunt you, the spirits will until you fall dead
   and your heart will stop.
E verything goes wrong in there, even for an armoured cop.
D readed Death omens walk the walls to search for the living

H appy you will be not, the only thing you will do is running
O h, we scream and yelp, that's all you'll do until you've gone.
U nited together, an army of ghosts.
S mall it's not, unbeatable it is.
E veryone will die one day and maybe this house
   is where you'll stay.

Matthew James (11)
Reepham Primary School

REDWALL RULES

R edwall is a huge red-stone Abbey.
E very creature who dwells there is kind and good.
D ibbuns play in the glorious sunshine.
W in, they always do against pretend enemies in battle,
A lthough the inhabitants are peaceful, there are those
    who defend the abbey well.
L everets, mice, voles and badgers live there
L ittle unhappiness swoops upon the dwellers.

R ats do not darken its doorways.
U nless the Redwallers are one warrior short,
L ong patrol hares always give a hand,
E very time they are patrolling in mossflower,
S ome but few, have unhappy moments within Redwall.

Rachel Staddon (10)
Reepham Primary School

A MILLENNIUM PRAYER

When I grow up I hope the world
Will be a better place
I hope the people won't get killed
And everyone will be safe.

I wish that all the animals
Sent from heaven above
Are cared for and looked after
By you Lord and your love.

Andrew Harding (9)
Reepham Primary School

Rats Are Great

R ats are great, but not everyone knows,
A dorable and cute from heads to toes,
T hey are loyal and kind pets for you and me,
S ometimes they're cheeky but they always give glee!

A dventurously snuggling down my bed,
R ats don't like to be kept in the shed,
E agerly they snuffle around the room

G etting into mischief, leaving a fume,
R ats cheer me up when I'm feeling down
E ven though they leave messages that are brown.
A ttempt to get your mum to buy one for you!
T hen you can share all this fun too!

Liberty Smith (10)
Reepham Primary School

A Millennium Prayer

When I grow up I hope the world
Will stop the fighting and wars,
And places sad like Kosovo
Will be no more.

I wish that cancer will be cured
And everyone will be safe
And we will live in harmony
Living Lord, in your faith.

Georgina Hardiment (8)
Reepham Primary School

THE HAUNTED HOUSE

H ell hath come and will forever stay.
A n exhilarating scream pierces my ear.
U nited ghosts reveal themselves.
N ever enter the house of demons,
T o be cursed by the Flying Dutchman.
E ver certain they were banished there,
D on't be foolish to fall for the crying.

H e who goes in will be forever dead,
O nly God and heaven could help us now
U nless the good defeat the cursed and bad.
S o follow my advice to the letter,
E ven if you are strong.

Kieran Delaney (10)
Reepham Primary School

MY SLEEPY CAT

S leepy little cat
L ying on my lap
E yes shut a'dreaming
E ars twitching and listening
P urring quietly and sweetly
Y awning sleepily and happily

C arefree and tired
A nd dreaming of wonders
T ired again, sleepy cat?

Alice Butler (10)
Reepham Primary School

HAUNTED HOUSE

H aunted house hiding in the woods
A mong the creepy trees it stood
U nder the roof where dead bodies lie
N ot daring to look with a single eye
T errifying sight of blood and bones
E choing noises sounding like groans
D eadly screams piercing my ears

H iding away from the bats in the air
O vergrown weeds come up from the ground
U gly spiders make no sound
S limy walls, mould too
E scaping is what I need to do.

Rosie Barwick (10)
Reepham Primary School

HALLOWE'EN

H orrible ghosts fly around
A scary place with no sound.
L ying there in my bed
L iving is pointless, I wish I was dead.
O ver my head an eye looked at me,
W herever I am, I should not be
E verywhere zombies lay,
E very night, every day,
N ever go in there, I always say.

Bruce Fielder (10)
Reepham Primary School

THE HAUNTED HOUSE

H orrifying ghosts rule the air,
A nd even the monster that has no hair.
U nder the cobwebbed tables of grim
N ever challenging skeletons, that are always so dim.
T his is the house that is so ghostly,
E ven the ghoulies are scared mostly.
D eath or petrify, which would you rather?

'H e looks as though he'll stay with his father.
O r maybe he'll stay with his mother.'
U nendlessly the ghosts speak together
S melling putrid smells, time to time
E ver would that house be mine?

Gemma Lambert (10)
Reepham Primary School

CREEPY CATS

C reeping along the pavement,
R ats scatter at each step.
E very night you go out hunting.
E agle eyes scanning the ground.
P eople stop to pet you in the daylight,
　 now it's a different world.
Y ou wander along the streets like a ghost.

C ats of all shapes and sizes are coming back home,
A nother night gone.
T omorrow it will happen again,
S ilently, you slide inside.

Ali Hewson (10)
Reepham Primary School

NIGHT-TIME

At night-time when the bright light has gone,
animals come out to play
while we humans lie in the world of dreams.
The owl hoots and toots, mice scuttle, running around
avoiding the owls' claws and squeaking.
The fox, sly is he, stalks the hen which perched she is.
He snaps at her, she squawks and send up the alarm,
the farmer runs out with a shotgun,
he shoots and kills the fox.
The hedgehog snuffles and scurries around
nibbling beetles as he runs along.
Then the bright light comes again and the animals
of the night are far away in the world of dreams,
where the night before we humans have been.

Lucy Ellena Johnson (11)
Seething & Mundham School

THOUSANDS

Diamonds last for eternity
Beneath, dreaming sleep rusts.
The sun and moon are heavily linked
Storms and winds rest in May
The sun rules in summer
And pines in winter.
The moon is all of souls.

Jack Ford (10)
Seething & Mundham School

THE SEA

The moon shone down upon it,
The seagulls rested on it.
> The sun it beat
> the glorious heat
> that glistened on the sea.

The dolphins swam beneath it.
The whales tried to keep it,
> but nothing living could control,
> the glory of the sea.

It's always ready and waiting.
It's used to people baiting
> small fish from under its beauty,
> the glory of the sea.

But soon they won't be there.
The sea will just lie bare
> its glory ripped, bit by bit,
> and people will just laugh at it,
> they can't surrender,
> they won't remember,
> the glory of the sea.

Jessie Elizabeth Hannah (11)
Seething & Mundham School

LIVERPOOL IS COMING HOME

Liverpool, Liverpool, win, win, win,
Score a goal and
Celebrate, celebrate, celebrate
Just celebrate.

Liverpool, Liverpool,
I like you,
So win, win, win.
So all the girls scream.

Joseph Stewart (9)
Seething & Mundham School

A JOURNEY FROM HARWICH TO HAMBURG

The boat slapped on the water
There was an explosion and
I was thrown from my bed.
The evil gale tossed the boat
Spinning it like a child's spinning top
He scraped his fingernails down the side of the boat,
'Sink boat, sink' he cried.
I looked out and saw his fierce eyes
Glaring, staring.
My heart beat faster
Then the gale climbed to the front of the boat
He saw the Captain
'Got you,' the gale spat at him
The Captain seemed to ignore him
So the gale went crazy -
Ripping
Tearing
Screaming
But it didn't have any effect
So the gale slunk off.

James Cossey (11)
Seething & Mundham School

Forest Of Enchantment

I've walked into a wonderland.
When I look up I can see shafts of
sunlight creeping through the canvas treetops.

The cool stream tickles my feet as I
jump on the slippery, stepping stones.
Fishes swim down the stream
scales glistening in the sunlight.
Suddenly something red catches my eye.
A little red fox cub jumps out of a bush
closely eyed by his mother.
I laugh to myself as I fall down into a
bed of clover to relive the
enchantment of this forest.

Charlotte Mowforth (11)
Seething & Mundham School

The Weather

The weather is so grand,
only when it's dry.
Hopefully it will snow so
we can make a snowman.
It might snow, it might be sunny,
who will ever know?

Matthew Smith (9)
Seething & Mundham School

GRANDAD AND ME IN THE PARK

Grandad and me in the park
doing handstands with a lark!
Grandad,
      Grandad
I couldn't live without him
Grandad,
      Grandad
I couldn't live without him
and here we are in the park
doing handstands with a
                  lark!

Eleanor Sieveking (8)
Seething & Mundham School

RACING CAR

A racing car goes zooming past.
I like them 'cause they are so fast,
The excitement going through the crowd,
Fades because the cars are loud.
But when the finish line is drawing in,
You feel as if you're going to win,
But when you stall inches away
You're like a child left astray.

Joe Carver (10)
Seething & Mundham School

MAN U

Through victory and defeat I've supported them through,
they're my favourite football team, they're called Man U.
Be the scorer Giggs or Nikki Butt, or the old great George Best,
they play at Old Trafford and should always win, I guess.

They play with class, well sometimes anyway,
one of my ambitions is just to see them play.
I'd love to get an autograph from one of their great stars,
or touch one of Beckham's posh expensive cars.

Their nickname's the 'Red Devils' although I'm not sure why,
when people are in the crowd, they shout out with a cry
'Come on you Reds, you can do it, you only have to try.'

Barry Kent (10)
Seething & Mundham School

FOOTBALL

Football, football is good,
Everybody's having fun.
We have won the FA Cup.
Let's all go to St James' Park.
We can do it all again.
Yes, we have done it again.

Steven Trudgill (9)
Seething & Mundham School

SCHOOL'S OUT

School's out, everyone's gone loopy
they're running around like mad.
What's wrong? What's the matter? It's only school.
Oh no, I forgot, summer hols are here.
I'd better start jumping around or people
will think I'm weird.
What am I going to do? I have no plans.
Quick, arrange something,
have a week's sleepover or something, *quick!*
Yes, I'm having a camp sleepover.

Hooray!

Emma Shipman (10)
Seething & Mundham School

FOX

He turned as the horn blew,
He ran for his life in the cold
Morning air.
He heard the barking and ran even
Faster to the hedge.
A streak of red fur.
He was struggling through as the
Thorns scratched him.
He ran over the road and into the
Field.
And then he felt the ice cold teeth
Going into him . . .

Matthew Butler (10)
Taverham Hall School

WOLF

I hear the cry but there is nothing
I can do but let him die
Stealthily I see it in the corner of
My eye, a wolf I cry.

I try to run, but it is like running on
Quick sand and my feet are tied
With a rubber band.

Help, I scream when I see its jaws
With blood dripping, I can't bear
The thought of skin ripping.

Just as it was about to devour my leg
I thought I heard blood dripping like
A shower.

I suddenly wake up, it was all
A dream so I feel my leg.

Sebastian Loxton (10)
Taverham Hall School

GHOSTS

Ghosts come in all shapes and sizes
There are big ones, small ones,
Fat ones, thin ones,
Some carry their heads under their arms
Some have axes through their heads.

Ghosts can be scary, some can't be scary,
Some like food,
Some like drink,
Some like being stupid.

There are many kinds of ghosts
But the most scariest ghosts are poltergeists
Or is it the bogeyman?
Nobody knows, but they're all around us.

Rupert Kenyon (10)
Taverham Hall School

THE SPITFIRE WAR

I took off from the runway,
I was in a world war,
This was not a bore.

I flew over the Channel
Of big sloshy waves,
If I crashed here, this would be my grave.

I suddenly saw some planes
I fired with my guns,
Some went down below me,
Others did a swerve.

Then I heard a bang!
It must of been my engine,
I was going down, I knew it.

Suddenly I woke up,
It must of been a dream,
It seemed all very strange
I wander how it must feel.

Alex Cooley (11)
Taverham Hall School

SCHOOL LIFE

The buzzer goes, we go into prayers,
My dear friend Seb faints, we stare,
'Come on everybody, coming through.'
'He is coming round.' I shouted.
At the end of prayers the announcements are made.
I got my hockey colours, hip, hip hooray!

We go to the first lesson.
It was maths, hooray.
I got out my book and began my sums.
Then I heard my name, I said, 'Yes Sir?' It was
Only the register,
The buzzer went, lesson two,
Geography, boo hoo!

Henry Sayer (11)
Taverham Hall School

THE MAGIC HORSE

In great splendour
It walks in the night
It is shiny and bright

It gallops through the night
It neighs behind the moon
It walks through the forest
And disappears so soon

I felt sad as if it was a friend
I climbed into bed and turned
Out the light.

Charlie Jones (9)
Taverham Hall School

THE FROG

The frog is green,
The frog is small,
The frog is seen
At the stall.

The frog likes water,
He swims very well,
He likes to linger
By the well.

His eyes are big,
His mouth is wide,
He loves moist places
Where he can hide.

The frog likes to hop,
He likes to jump around,
Look closely at the lily pond,
There he may be found.

He has a friend,
His name is Toad,
They have days out
Hopping down the road.

Ribitt, Ribitt, Ribitt,
The frog is saying goodbye,
Where is he going?
He's going to catch a fly.

Shelley Gabriel (8)
Taverham Hall School

UNICORN

He stands in trees,
As still as stone,
The wind is tossing his mane,
As he gallops through a field nearby,
His tail up swishing in the air,
As he flies up, up and away,
Over the moonlit sky,
Across the moon his shadow appears,
Like a diamond in a field,
His wings open like fire,
His horn sparkles like silver,
When he comes to land,
His hooves clatter against the cobbled stones,
I tell my mum but she won't believe me,
I tell my dad but he won't believe me,
So I don't tell anyone about him,
I keep it all to myself.

Jessica Turner (10)
Taverham Hall School

MONEY

Up, up and away,
I wish I could earn a thousand a day,
I'd spend it all on toys,
Like big toys for boys,
Especially on Yamaha bikes,
When I have nothing left,
I'd wish again, again and again.

William Drewery (9)
Taverham Hall School

Mrs Brand

Watch out! Watch out! Mrs Brand's about!
Her brown eyes stare from chair to chair.
Watch out! Watch out! Mrs Brand's about!
She always glares in a moonlight stare,
Her eyes flash with a distant crash.
She shouts and shouts at William Harris,
Before he's even out the door.
Watch out! Watch out! Mrs Brand's about!
Her wizard touch makes you quake with fright!
At the end of the day you will see,
A glimpse of a broomstick flying up, up and away!
In the morning she comes *back*.
Fire comes out, it keeps coming out.
When will it stop?
She grabs me by the hair
And throws me down the stairs.
She dresses up like a person in mourning.
But not a funeral in sight.
That witch! That witch!
Watch out! Watch out! Mrs Brand's about!
With her pointed hat, she looks a fright,
Her sandy hair falls down.
She thinks it's a crown.
She is coming near me now!
Put your name on your sheet,
Knowing you, you'll cheat!

R M Cooke (9)
Taverham Hall School

GHOSTS!

One creepy-crawly night,
Creepy weepy night.
The ghost of revenge
Was released out of the picture.

The ghost was creepy,
Scary witch was out haunting
For the night.
I was fast asleep.

When I heard a weird noise
I woke up.
Suddenly there was a boom!
I had a jump.

The last sound was ahhh!

Jamie Hambidge (10)
Taverham Hall School

SANDWICH

I like my sandwich in all kinds of flavours,
Such as banana and crisps,
Jam and that's not it,
Peanut butter and ham.

I like my sandwich in all kinds of breads,
Such as crusty, french, white, brown and thick,
And that's not it.

I like my sandwich in any way
As long as it doesn't give me a stomach ache!

Thomas Burrows (8)
Taverham Middle School

THE DOOR

Go and open the door
Maybe outside there's
A bulb, or a stalk,
A flower
Or a wood.

Go and open the door
Maybe there's a tunnel
That seems to get longer
And longer.

Go and open the door
If there's a dog at your feet
It will go.

Go and open the door
Even if it's a dark cave,
Even if there's fire all around you
Go and open the door.

At least
You have tried.

Kenneth O'Neill (9)
Taverham Middle School

THE MAGIC BOX

I will put in my box;
A cobra with poisonous teeth
Predator boots that make you go as fast as a speeding bullet,
A leopard as fast as a cheetah.

I will put in my box;
All the Man U team,
Uzi with such powerful bullets it could kill 5 men
With one shot.
A dinosaur with shining sharp teeth.
A shark as strong as 100 men.

My box is fashioned from;
Gold and silver coins, diamonds from the far North
Of the South Pole,
Blood from the insides of a T-Rex's heart,
I shall wrestle the cobra,
Kill the dinosaurs,
Dribble past Jaap Stam!

Taylor Hale (9)
Taverham Middle School

MY MAGIC BOX

I will put in my box:
The sparkling magic of the God of the Sun,
The golden boots of Michael Owen
And the gold of the Sun.

I will put in my box:
The shine of silver,
The gold of a sparkling star
And the black of the dark skies.

My box is made from the
Most sparkling rock,
From the moon and its hinges
Are made from magic.

In my box I shall fly out of
The solar system and back.
I will go to every England match
They play.

Stuart Baldwin (8)
Taverham Middle School

MAGIC BOX

I will put in the box;
The first leaf which falls in autumn,
A roar of a lion,
And over a hundred pounds
I will put in the box,
A touch of frost in my hand,
A unicorn as beautiful as can be,
And the silver moon
I will put in the box;
The sparkle of the Sun,
The tooth of the dragon,
The howl of a wolf at full Moon.
My box is fashioned from;
Diamonds as shiny as the Sun
With moon rocks to decorate it.
I shall play in my box
With a snow tiger as white as can be.

Emily Morgan (9)
Taverham Middle School

THE MAGIC BOX

I will put in the box;
A beautiful glittering white horse,
The noise of the crowd as Michael Owen scores,
A glittering, shiny, silver moon.
I will put in my box;
My favourite pop group,
All of the most wonderful fizzy drinks,
Every golden World Cup trophy.
My box is fashioned from;
Glittering gold,
Silver steel
And shiny shells from the corners.
In my box I shall play a football match against Michael Owen.

Stephanie Rhodes (9)
Taverham Middle School

SCHOOL TIME

I know when it's school time,
Because I hear the church bells chime.
I run along the street.
As I pass the field of wheat
I hurry along,
As I sing my favourite song.
In the distance I see my friends play football,
As I pass the old city wall.
I'm there, I see my friends play,
As I see horses grazing in the hay.

Ben Gray (9)
Taverham Middle School

THE GREEK LEGEND

Zeus, mighty Zeus
Hurls down thunderbolts in his rage.
Hera, Hera wife of Zeus
Goddess of marriage, plus having her skin beige.

Apollo and Helios, Gods of the Sun
Riding the chariot across the sky.
Poseidon, the God with a trident
Lord of the sea and doesn't lie.

Hades, Lord of death like Pluto
Ruling the grimly underworld.
Heracles, the son of great God Zeus
Killing monsters on the Earth, our world.

Hephaestus, God of fire
Who cut open Zeus's head, the great Athena then emerged.
Athena was the Goddess of war like Ares
Ares loved Aphrodite and Ares urged.

Bacchus the God of wine born from Semele
Who met King Midas.
Artemis, Goddess of the Moon and hunting
Deer drawn chariot Artemis has.

Dione and Uranus, the sky, gave birth to Aphrodite
Goddess of love and beauty
All the good greek legends.

Samuel Ashley (8)
Taverham Middle School

THE MAGIC BOX

I will put in my box;
Big bags of chocolate cream cakes,
A James Bond suit.
A bullet flashing gun.

I will put in my box;
A real live light brown cuddly teddy
Which talks to me.
A bed made out of shiny gold.
Lots of footballs as well.

My box is fashioned from;
Gold that is curved, it says 'Football mad'.
The hinges are made out of children's knuckles.

I shall;
Play football with the England team,
Win 12-0,
I shall get all of the autographs.

Nick Hazell (9)
Taverham Middle School

THE WRITER OF THIS POEM

The writer of this poem
Is as bold as a boxer,
As amazing as an acrobat,
As aggressive as an adder.

As silly as a clown,
As bouncy as a bouncy ball,
As bright as the Sun,
As smart as a scientist.

As healthy as a football player,
As sporty as Michael Owen,
As bubbly as a bubble bath,
As successful as his dad.

The writer of this poem,
Although he's very smart,
His last name is Scarff,
And he's rubbish at art.

Andrew Scarff (9)
Taverham Middle School

THE MAGIC BOX

I will put in my box;
The greenest meadows and the bluest seas,
The magic of the Sun as it sets upon the calm sea.
The strangest jewels from all over the world.

I will put in the box;
The stars which sparkle, all the moons from space,
A crowd of ponies which toss their manes,
A warm cosy pool which stretches for miles.

My box is fashioned from
Rubies and shells with stars on the lid,
Silver and gold which shine like mad,
On the side is the bright sun which lights it up.

In my box I shall
Ride on a camel across a burning desert,
And eat off a gummy gum tree,
I shall drink the strangest water.

Poppy Savage (8)
Taverham Middle School

THE READER OF THIS POEM

The reader of this poem
Is as tall as a tree
As smelly as a sock
As brightly coloured as a bee.

As giggly as a monkey
As daring as a sky flyer
As bouncy as a wallaby
As boring as a donkey.

As tricky as a butterfly
As chatty as a chatterbox
As fat as a pig
As spiteful as a bumblebee.

The reader of this poem
Always sleeps on the floor
But the reader of this poem
Is as boring as a bore!

Fionna McLauchlan (9)
Taverham Middle School

THE MAGIC BOX

I will put in my box;
The wonderful blue skies above
The glittering Moon and Sun
The sparkling stars.

I will put in the box;
The most beautiful gem in the world
The golden sands
And the blue seas.

My box is fashioned from
All kinds of shells,
My birth stone
And rocks.

I shall
Sunbathe and get a golden tan,
Sleep as long as I can
And swim for miles.

Stephanie Coker (9)
Taverham Middle School

THE MAGIC BOX

I will put in the box;
The smoothest and best pieces of jade,
Amber as well,
All the precious stones in the world.

I will put in the box;
Sparkling diamonds,
Magic crystals
And beautiful rocks.

My box is fashioned from;
The best sparkling pieces of jade,
Yellow amber shells as well.

I shall go down to the deep ocean
And find pieces of jade.

Jade Powell (8)
Taverham Middle School

THE DEATH BOX

I will put in the box;
A scream of terror from the bulging capes
A shiver of cold from the darkest woods,
A howl from a wolf that will spread terror.

I will put in the box;
A dragon that has a reign of hatred,
Two goblins that will eat human flesh,
The rumbling roar from a grizzly bear.

My box is fashioned from;
Freezing cold ice with a hint of death,
Its hinges are made from a child's knucklebones,
It is decorated with ink that is blood.

I shall become king of all these terrors,
Name myself Mr Death and darkness,
Have two pet wolves that drink blood instead of water.

Aaron Hunter (8)
Taverham Middle School

PAPER

Plain or lined, coloured and strong
Different sizes if you go wrong
You have to rub or cross things out
Which sometimes make you scream
And shout
It gives you cuts like swords and knives
And people think it can destroy their lives
A threatening message that they won't survive.

Aaron Cooper (11)
Wensum Middle School

THE GREAT GIANT

The great giant
eats lots of people
mean, angry, ugly
like a rock crumbling
away
like a bean rolling
around
it makes me feel
tiny
like a centipede
that no one notices
the giant reminded us
that we are not the
must important
things in the world.

Marc Woodcock (11)
Wensum Middle School

DOLPHIN

A water glider
A fast spider
A playful creature
A sea feature
A piece of shiny glass
A very wavy piece of grass
A sea burning piece of rubber
A crystal deep under cover
A blade slicing the sea
An eye as far as you can see
A rubbery bouncy ball
A gentle creature, an example to us all.

Carla Moore (10)
Wensum Middle School

DOLPHIN DREAMS

A diving thing
in a ring
Shining blue
It might sing for you
Bashing the sea
Like a lion with a tree
Splashing
Dashing
Splash
Splash
Splash
Splash.

Katie Lain-Rogers (11)
Wensum Middle School

THE SKY

The sky
Up, up, high,
Silky, starry and shiny,
As beautiful as a jewelled gown.
Like a huge silk cloth protecting the Earth.
It makes me feel small,
As small as an ant that nobody can see.

The sky
It seems to glow at night.

Kalwinder Digpal (11)
Wensum Middle School

BASKETBALL

This is a round thing
Bouncy as a frog.
It's as rough as concrete
Ripply lines on it like the sea.
Makes me feel like I can fly
A round circle ever going
As round as a clock.
Blue like the sea
Bounces on the floor
Scores goals.

Luke Wilson (11)
Wensum Middle School

WHAT AM I?

A boat carrier
A land barrier
A land eater
A lake meeter
A meander maker
A flooder of acres
A silent mover
A big hoover
What am I?

Liessa Moy (11)
Wensum Middle School

THE SECRET ANIMAL

A cuddly thing
 A little king
A nibbling creature
 A lovely feature
A dandylion snatcher
 A nasty catcher
A little digger
 A mischief trigger.

Gemma Howes (10)
Wensum Middle School

THE SECRET CREATURE

A colourful rainbow in the sky,
A fluttering creature flying by,
A pair of wings,
With patterned strings,
A lily pad,
It's feeling sad,
But now it has gone away
And it'll come back another day.

Katrina Berry (11)
Wensum Middle School

GUESS WHO?

Cat bait
Nibble a cake
Cheese stealer
Exercise wheeler
White and grey heap of fur
Sometimes he eats cucumber
His nick-name is Spark plug
He sleeps in his cage, nice and snug
He has needle sharp teeth
And has fur as long as a sheep
Bottle sucker
Sawdust roller
Eye drooper
A real trooper
Cat tormentor
Furry, food storer
Carrot muncher
Bar chewer
Blue eyes
Amazed by flies.

Kirsty Hinde (10)
Wensum Middle School

RIVERS

Long and bendy
Short and stretchy
Runs for miles
Lots of spirals
Nets and rods
Bits and bobs
Fish and pollution
What's the solution?

Daniel Bird (10)
Wensum Middle School

OUT IN ORBIT

Whirling, swirling about in the air,
The moon and stars are so sweet.
On go our weighted boots and spacesuits.

Zooming, zooming into space I go,
I feel terrified.
Whizzing, leaping, flying about,
Oxygen tanks on they go.
I really want to go home.

We change our minds.
Off, off, go our spacesuits.
Home, home I go!

Elizabeth Dewsbury (9)
Woodland View Middle School

MY EXCITING TRIP TO SPACE

I looked around in space
I saw my rocket
It made me feel bad.
When I saw my home on Earth it made me feel sad.
When I started floating around, guess what?
I saw a wonderful view of nine planets!
I saw Saturn, Uranus, Mars, Venus, Earth, Mercury,
Pluto and Neptune!
I saw Venus with all its gasses.
Mars, all red.
I saw Earth, with water and land green and blue.
I felt excited.
My heart tingled.
My fingers, they jingled!
Next I leapt very far.
Next I saw a shooting star.
Then I decided I'd go back to Earth, I was bored.
So I climbed in my rocket.
Got ready to go.
Off I went.
I was travelling around.
I was nearly home.
I couldn't wait.
I would have a lovely tea on a big round plate!
What a wonderful day in space.

Emma Dodds (8)
Woodland View Middle School

FRIENDS

I wait for you every day
To come and give me my lush hay.
You give me an apple or two,
And I'll do anything you want me to.

Then you'll select my tack,
And take me for a nice long hack,
We'll gallop through the grass,
Dodging anything we pass.

We return home,
You get my comb,
And you give me a good rub down,
I love you so much, but when you pull my
Tangles I frown.

When you give me a pat,
And hang up your riding hat,
I bend my head,
Knowing that I'm going to bed,
When you go I'm full of sorrow,
But know you'll come back tomorrow.

Michele Perry (11)
Woodland View Middle School

UP, UP AND AWAY

The wonderful sensation of drifting away,
The feeling of tightness,
The feeling of air,
As I go up, up and away.

As I calmly float away, float away,
It's like the flutter of a bird,
It's like the whisper of the wind,
As I go up, up and away.

Scott Kelly (11)
Woodland View Middle School

THE GHOST RIDER

The wind was a howling, wolf running
around the leafless trees.
The moon was a pale ghost kneeling down
on its funny knees.
The road was a ribbon of long tape glittering
in the moon.
And the ghost rider came galloping,
galloping, galloping.
And the ghost rider came galloping up to
his room.
The ghost rider was howling loudly in the
moonlight tonight.
Riding around in the dark and giving us all
such a fright.
The ghost rider came out to ride when the
night was dark.
His horse was as big as a tree.
It really scared me!
I ran away as fast as I could from the scary
park.

Gemma Holmes (10)
Woodland View Middle School

THE DEEP BLUE SEA

The sea, the sea,
What wonders it holds,
The crashing of waves,
And the beauty of old,
It rustles and clangs like an old tin whistle,
While sounding as if it's been hurt by a thistle.

The sea is calm,
Not a sound anywhere,
Until a ship sails over there,
It makes waves as big as a house,
For children it's fun but not for a mouse.

The reef's full of life,
And the sea's full of coral,
It reminds me of a very good moral,
It tells you how pollution is bad,
And how to stop it before we are sad.

Nicholas Taylor (11)
Woodland View Middle School

SUNSET

S   un light beams, shimmering on the sea
U   nder the sun the people lie on the beach.
N   ightly the sun goes down.
S   and shines as the sun goes down.
E   very bird is going to sleep until the new day.
T   urtles go in their burrow.

Daniel Smith (11)
Woodland View Middle School

UP, UP AND AWAY

Up, up and away
In a rocket,
What is that I see?
A flying comet,
Some shooting stars,
Maybe, the planet Mars,
What else is that I see?
Earth
Up, up and away.

Up, up and away,
In a hot air balloon,
What is that I see?
Very small people,
Maybe, my house,
Where am I?
In the Sky
Up, up and away.

Up, up and away,
In the world of dreams,
What is that I see?
Big fluffy clouds,
Maybe, some singing birds,
Where am I?
Heaven
Up, up and away.

Nikki Wilby (11)
Woodland View Middle School

The Millennium

Just before the clock strikes twelve
We say goodbye to the last century.
We count down 10, 9, 8, only a few
Seconds to wait.
7, 6, 5, people are waiting for it
4, 3, 2, people are pouring champagne
1, the new millennium is here!

People are so excited
As they drink champagne
Until they are legless.

The day after the fun
Everyone has a hangover
There is a mountain of rubbish
Really high,
Which nearly touches the sky.

Jason Simpson (12)
Woodland View Middle School

Snakes

The slithering serpent
The coiled friend
The choking rope
The biting blade.

Large but elegant
Small but swift
With skin of many colours.

Among the lush
Rain forest foliage
This pure bred hunter lies
So easily concealed.

He waits
And waits
Then pounces with all his might
Upon his prey
Who is riddled with fright.

James Finch (11)
Woodland View Middle School

THE MILLENNIUM FIREWORK

Voices cheer and people pour the wine,
There is so much noise, nobody hears
Me zoom up into the sky.
How come you're so lucky to be able
To have a long life.
Ours only starts and ends at the
Same time.
I am made up of bright colours,
As I burst open my heart flutters,
I see my family and friends,
Just as our lives end.

The Millennium night is all over,
My life has ended so fast,
It is the start to a new Millennium
I wish my life could last.

Sophie Allen (12)
Woodland View Middle School

THE BIRTHDAY CAKE MY DOG ATE

The birthday cake
my dog ate
was special for my
dad,
It was his fortieth birthday
and he was rather proud.

The cake had berries and cream and sponge inside,
My dog just jumped and landed beside, he sniffed
and sniffed and then he grinned.

You could hear a gobble then a gulp, then a crunch.
My dog had eaten my dad's speciality birthday cake.

Natasha Gladden (12)
Woodland View Middle School

WINTER POEM

I got up in the morning,
What a shock I had!
The snow had fallen,
The snowflakes fell down, down,
Glittering in the sunrise.
I asked Mum to let me out,
I made several snowmen.
Mum said 'We're going to town
To do our shopping.'
The car doors were frozen,
So Dad was on the case!

Edward Allison (8)
Woodland View Middle School

WINTER

In the seasons always sneezing
Winter is the best
Snowing, hailing, cooking meals,
Lovely and tasty, yum! yum! yum!

Cold outside, warm indoors
In the snow or on the go
Waiting or wailing, I don't know
But have to go in the snow.

Icy and cold in the pond
Warm and snug in your bed
Heat, meat, lovely wheat
Go on, go on have a snack to eat.

Dull, misty, windy, white,
As white as snow and as black as night
Don't be scared on the ice
Slippery and sliding
Oh no! I'm flat.

Don't worry I'm here.
Go to bed and don't care.
In the morning snug as a rug
In the snow it's fun to see
Go and play but don't sneeze.
Achew!

Siobhan Allen (8)
Woodland View Middle School

GHOSTS

Sometimes ghosts are friendly,
Sometimes ghosts give scares,
Ghosts within the hallways,
Ghosts upon the stairs.

Sometimes ghosts are scary,
Sometimes ghosts aren't there,
Ghosts within the graveyards,
Ghosts up in their lairs.

Sometimes ghosts are powerful,
Sometimes ghosts aren't tough,
Ghosts within the colossal cornfields,
Ghosts not out of puff.

So now all the ghosts have gone to sleep,
You should understand,
Ghosts aren't really that bad at all,
Be careful Martian's might land.

When all the ghosts wake up again,
You should rightfully know,
I must finish here, I heard a loud noise,
Oh no, whoa boy whoa!

Mathew Galea (12)
Woodland View Middle School

SWIRLING, TWIRLING

All around floating high,
small stars, big sky, planets,
boulders high in the sky.
I wish I could stay high above the ground.

Whizzing, twirling, swirling high,
turning round above the ground.
Wish I could stay dancing, prancing around
above the ground.
I don't want to waste the day away!

Leanne Finch (8)
Woodland View Middle School

AROUND THE TABLE!

Around the table in my living room,
at 20 to 12 at night,
we all sat patiently as well as the dog,
and not a pin drop could be heard.
Around the table in my living room,
at a quarter to 12 at night,
still waiting for the clock to strike 12,
and letting the minutes go by.
Around the table in my living room,
at 10 to 12 at night,
running around in a circle to keep warm at night.
Around the table in the living room,
at 5 to 12 at night,
worn out and breathless
and desperate for a drink.
Around the table in my living room,
at 12 o'clock at night,
ding, dong, the clock has finally struck
now it is the Millennium 2000!

Lisa Beaumont (12)
Woodland View Middle School

THE ROOM WITH A THOUSAND PICTURES

The room has lots of pictures all over the walls,
There are small ones, big ones, round ones and square ones,
There are pictures of people, dogs and maps,
Some are photographs, some are paintings.

There are family pictures and friend pictures,
Some old, some new and some black and white,
On some there is a mixture of people and others are just singles,
All represent memories of all things in the past.

There are pictures of my cousins, pictures of my grandma,
Pictures of my nana, aunts and uncles,
Pictures of my mum and dad, pictures of my brother and sister,
And pictures of *me*!

There are pictures of holidays, weddings and family get togethers,
There are school pictures, pictures of me as a baby,
Paintings of London in olden times and a tapestry to welcome my
Brother,
All of these mean a lot to me as they are in my *front room*.

Sarah Bird (12)
Woodland View Middle School

UP, UP AND AWAY!

I was up in my rocket,
With a camera in my pocket,
Happy and excited,
Guess what I had sighted?

It was a seven-headed creature,
With another nasty feature.
A boiling, bubbling wart,
So I screamed, 'Mission abort!'

Down I quickly dropped,
As my ears popped.
I landed on the Earth
In the arms of Papa Smurf!

Alan Warner (11)
Woodland View Middle School

I CLOSE MY EYES AND DREAM

I close my eyes and dream that I am floating in the sky,
Round and round with lots and lots of yummy, tasty pies.
Slowly the pies disappear and something flies into my ear.
As I go to pick it out,
I look down and give a shout!
I am really high in the sky, way above the ground,
When, out of the blue, I hear a rumbling sound.
Oh no! Here comes an aeroplane, flying straight for me!
No, it's just my tummy wishing it had eaten all its tea!
Slowly the sky gets darker, so I leap from my hot air balloon,
Out into a rocket ship heading for the moon!
I look out of the window and then I have a fright,
I see a spaceman on the loo heading out of sight!
Quickly I grab him and pull him in,
But he starts to disappear, so I jump from the rocket,
Back to the balloon.
Then, all of a sudden, I wake up
And find myself on the floor of my room!
I climb into my bed again and . . .
I close my eyes and dream that I am floating in the sky,
Round and round with lots and lots of yummy pies!

Samantha Lake (12)
Woodland View Middle School

ON MARS

In space there are nine planets,
I'm on one of those.
The planet I'm on is quite hot.
I am on Mars you know.
It has these craters.
Deep and red.
It's very odd you know!
The stars and moon look far away
When it's only a thousand miles.
I'm whizzing round.
I feel sick!
I'm bouncing up,
Hardly touching the surface.
What I can see is amazing!

Jack Taylor (8)
Woodland View Middle School

LEAPING IN SPACE!

I'm leaping around,
I'm having fun,
Seeing the planets and seeing the sun.
The moon is big,
The stars are small,
The sky is tall.
Some of the planets are very cool.
Seeing space is the best,
Better than any of the rest!

Charlotte Morgan (9)
Woodland View Middle School

ZOOMING IN SPACE

Zooming in space
Going into orbit
Spinning around
Boots burning and puffing
The speed's amazing
1000 miles an hour
Zooming in space.

Breaking the speed limit
Chasing comets
Landing on the moon
Zooming past satellites!
Zooming space . . . is wonderful.

Thomas Field (9)
Woodland View Middle School

THE REALLY COLD DAY

As the breeze whistles through the trees and
                                        made them rattle,
As the snow falls down on the ground,
As the animals stay in their homes,
As animals hibernate in the winter,
As paths are covered with snow,
As people walk and make footprints,
As birds sing in the trees, saying
'It's cold, it's cold.'

Thomas Grint (8)
Woodland View Middle School

WINTER'S COMING

Winter's coming, better get ready, better get dressed.
Frost, cold, snow and freeze will soon be here.
I'm so excited.
I love skating on the icy rink.
Sparkling, glittering, splat goes the snow.
Whistling past, the wind will always go.
Oh I don't know, I'm feeling dull and misty
Robin sings his merry melody,
Tweet tune.
I'm cold, I'm cold.
But I'll soon be warm for spring is coming.

Jordan Hare (8)
Woodland View Middle School

WINTER WONDERLAND

In my winter wonderland, everything is nice.
Icicles hanging everywhere,
Cold, as cold as ice.
Ice skating on the pond
As we watch the ice sparkle.
We make a snowman and play snowballs,
Then we hear our friends call.
We all play together,
Laughing, having fun,
We can all say the snow is *fun!*

Charlotte Leeming (9)
Woodland View Middle School

WINTER

On the coldest winter
morning
snow started to fall
in big round balls.
I got out my winter
clothes and wellies.
My feet crunching
along the falling snow.
Icicles hanging from
every window.
Crunching, crunching
along the snow.
Crispy leaves
along the ground,
crisp, crisp, crisp,
snow still falling.

Sarah Wilson (8)
Woodland View Middle School

GLITTERING SNOW

The snow is glittering.
When I walk in the glittering snow, it goes 'crunch.'
The pond is sparkling and it's glistening,
I don't want to break it.
My mum tells me to come,
I don't want to go away from the glittering snow.
The snow is too cold.
I go in a bush and duck down,
My mum's gone in.

Emma Waters (9)
Woodland View Middle School

MY EXCITING WINTER

On the 1st of December
I put on my wellies
And went outside.
It was freezing cold,
My pond had turned
Into ice.

I went up closer,
It was solid,
I trod on it,
It cracked!
I was terrified.
I built a snowman,
It was fun,
I was getting cold,
So I went in.

Adam White (9)
Woodland View Middle School

THE SNOWMAN

I am cold,
Then I walk in the cold snow.
It is a blizzard.
I made a snowman,
My friends made a snowman too.
My friends and I were cold,
The snow is white and icy.

Kerry Locke (9)
Woodland View Middle School

A Trip To The Moon

On the launch pad,
Staring at the rocket.
Step forwards.
Door opens as you go inside.
All the flashing lights as it starts to take off,
Excited, proud to get this far.
As you reach orbit, you float,
Doing somersaults,
Bouncing, dancing about.
As you reach the moon with all its humps and bumps,
You see asteroids floating about.

As you land on that dark, damp moon,
You see an alien in a big balloon.
You jump up and freak out
With a glass of soda.
You go back to Earth like a flash of lightning!

Hazel Pointer (8)
Woodland View Middle School

Magic Butterfly

Tiny creature you may be,
Bringing joy to all who see.
Dancing, prancing without care,
Darting, diving, here and there.
Floating, fluttering up on high,
Soaring, shimmering in the sky.
You . . . the magic butterfly.

Fern Wilkinson (12)
Woodland View Middle School

The Filing Cabinet Monstrosity

Its tall shadow looms over the classroom
Blocking out all the sunlight
What a sight!

It chases you around the classroom with a stapler,
Hits you with erasers,
Puts ink on your school work, hides your homework,
Crinkles the edges and covers it with dirt.

It eats staples for breakfast,
Your lunch for brunch,
Blue-tack for lunch,
And with a mighty crunch, chews pins for tea.

Some days, on rainy days, but usually on Mondays
It grows legs and chases you around the playground,
Steals the footballs,
Joins in with netball,
And eats the rugby balls,

Hides all the school bags and turns around in old rags.

Calum Awcock (11)
Woodland View Middle School

A Madagascan Rayed Tortoise

Slow as a slug,
Not a bug,
Has a shell,
A tortoise.

He comes from Madagascar,
He is a rayed tortoise,
Every day is like a year to him,
Every year must be a century to him.

A rare species of his kind,
Fascinating shell patterns,
How is the shell decorated?
Only he knows!

His class is reptila
His family are testudinidae
His order is chelonia
And his name is tortoise!

Stephen Dewsbury (12)
Woodland View Middle School

ON THE MOON

On the Moon it is like a rock.
Floating around in a space suit is quite fun.
On the moon there are mountains that look like cheese.
It's lovely to be an astronaut
But you cannot tease!
Whizzing through the air
Then something caught my eye,
I had to stare,
I felt a bit frightened
Then I felt quite sad
Suddenly I felt glad.

I was then jumping about
I saw an alien with a big snout!
The stars are silver,
As bright as they could be.
I realised the alien was a he!
Leaping is the word
Then I saw an alien called Heard.

Emmaleigh Webb
Woodland View Middle School

FIREWORKS

F   lashing, dashing past my feet
I   see a sudden explosion
R   ight, left, then up and down
E   xciting fireworks flashing to the earth
W   orking hard to get set up then suddenly a bang here and whoosh
     there
O   range, yellow and red
R   ocking backwards and forwards from side to side
K   een and eager children watching the bonfire flicker
S   uddenly the last firework goes up and it finishes and when you look
     around you've still got stars in your eyes.

Michelle Godfrey (11)
Woodland View Middle School

THE TREE

Shining leaves that glow,
Flashing strobe lights blow,
Darkness down below,
The soft and furry bark goes down into the dark.
The person inside the tree is as beautiful as you and me.
The branches sway and glint into the moonlight, soon it
will be winter,
The tree will shed its leaves like tears,
The rain will come apouring and the sun will disappear.

Roxanne Coleman (11)
Woodland View Middle School

THE SMUGGLER

The wind was a howling wolf running around the leafless trees,
The moon was a pale ghost kneeling down on its trembling knees,
The road was an old slithering, shiny, hissing, scaly snake,
And the smuggler came riding,
Riding - riding,
The smuggler came riding up to the old dark lake.

The smuggler had a red, flappy, thin, long cloak tied round his neck,
His friends were called James, Jamie, Tom, Charlie, Conner, Ben and
Fleck,
The smuggler was going very fast now, 'Hurry up.' he said,
He fell off his horse and said, 'Ouch.'
'Shh!' said his friends,
They went into a house and found a pencil with lead.

They took the pencil from the pot and said, 'Look what we have found.'
He picked it up suddenly, it fell with a 'Clash' to the ground,
'Shh, Shh!' The owners woke with a start, the smugglers quickly hid,
'Shh!' The smugglers hid quietly,
Quiet, quiet,
The smuggler got free and his escape was rapid.

Suzanne Godfrey (9)
Woodland View Middle School

SPIDERMAN

There once was a man from Cider
Who ate a big, black spider,
He grew eight legs,
And two big heads,
Got on his knees and said *'Help me!'*

Daniel Green (12)
Woodland View Middle School

RAIN

Raindrops are like little pearls
Falling off the rooftops
Overtaking each other,

A raindrop is like a shimmering, racing car
Speeding down the windowpane,

Cold rain is like a shiny pearl
That trickles down the window, forming streams,

Raindrops are like the speeding missiles racing
Down the window frame,

Raindrops are like a glimmering rainbow
Falling from the sky,

A raindrop is like a shooting star speeding
Like an aeroplane.

Lee Bevis (9)
Woodland View Middle School

WINTER SHIVERS

Winter's mainly cold, dark too.
Gardens covered in snow.
You mainly get snow in December.
Snow ball fights everywhere!
Snowflakes falling from the sky.
Warm fire indoors.
Tucked up in bed nice and warm.

Peter Berryman (8)
Woodland View Middle School

SPACE

All was quiet and dark.
The fiery sun burning.
The brightly coloured planets dazzling away.
The wonderful mountains on the moon.
Our magnificent galaxy, the Milky Way.
The nine planets sparkling brightly,
Uranus, Saturn and Neptune with their gleaming rings.
Neil Armstrong the first man to land on the moon in 1969.
Shooting stars flying across the dark sky.
Giant rockets taking off from their massive launch pads.
Twinkling stars in the fantastic black sky.
Space shuttles zooming through space.
Wonderful, ever expanding, infinite.

Space!

Craig Inman (9)
Woodland View Middle School

FLOATING IN THE SKY

Floating in the starry sky
It is really a beautiful sight.
The rocket goes bang and the suit goes squawk.
The icy moon glimmers in the sunlight.
The stars ping and gleam in the deep dark sky as
The sun sparkles.
As I look down at rocky mountains
There are rocks like fountains.
I got to the space ship
It is very slow,
Home we go!

Daniel Dack (9)
Woodland View Middle School

THE BLIZZARD BITES

Winter is coming with a biting blizzard
It's almost here.
It's coming soon.
You can feel it in the air.
When morning comes it brings the blizzard.
The snow lashes against the window.
I'm stuck indoors.
Time passes slowly,
At last it stops.
A chance to play outside,
The biting blizzard feels as sharp as knives against
My cheeks.
Soon they glow red as roses.
After making my snowman my fingers and toes feel
Like blocks of ice.
I return indoors.
A mug of hot tea soon thaws me out.
Sit by the fire.
I feel sad - soon winter will be over.
The sun will return.
My snowman will melt and the biting blizzard will be
Gone once more.

Charlotte Last (9)
Woodland View Middle School

UP, UP AND AWAY

Flying up, up in the air
Like a plane or a bird
Wishing I could fly up high
Just like a dragonfly.

I want to go into space
So I can see gory aliens
To see Saturn, Mars and the moon
Trying and trying to get away.

Theo Chamberlin (10)
Woodland View Middle School

SPACE SICK

I feel sick, I'm going purple
My head is spinning round in circles.

Help me! Help me!
I've lost my shoe.
Thank you! Thank you!
Can I go to the loo?

Ouch! That's my head,
Now I really feel like going to bed.

Pluto, Venus, loads of stars
Uranus, moon . . .
Look, there's Mars.

Up in space I think I see
Nothing much, just a galaxy . . .

But then again, it's quite fun
I think it was made just as time had begun.

Up in space I feel very proud
But one problem . . . there isn't a single cloud.

Up in space I think I'm flying
But sometimes I think I'm dying!

Karl Curson (9)
Woodland View Middle School

SPACE

Whooooooosh!
Our country,
Our sky,
Our Earth,
Space!
Space is black,
Space has our Earth,
Space has no gravity,
Space has no oxygen.
You may see mini mountains,
Just on the Moon.
The sun shines on us,
And lights up our days.
Mars, as red as beetroot,
Only in the darkness of space.
It never stops growing,
Like you and me,
With all nine planets,
In our solar system.
And Neil Armstrong,
Having such strong arms,
To go to the Moon,
In the dark sky all around him.
That is *space!*

Paul Barker (9)
Woodland View Middle School

WANTED WINTER

Winter is coming
It's just around the corner
Frosty and stiff
Gradually ice icicles forming
Icicles as sharp as a sword
Ice skiddy, wild wind,
As cold as the North Pole
As white as snow
Shivering snow
As cold as fridges
It's cold and chilly,
Trees white, roads white
Gates white and white.
Every body is happy
Now the snow is here.

Michael Cowles (8)
Woodland View Middle School

SAD SEALS

I always see them performing
Doing tricks, dancing, eating fish
But I always wonder what life's like for them.
If they're happy or melancholy to be there.
In the cage or in the pool, sad, bored, not being
Able to live a normal life.
Just because we caught them and took them to a
Strange location.
Away from the sea and the beach,
Their home.

Matthew Moon (10)
Woodland View Middle School

SPACE

In the Milky Way we have a blinding sun
It's amazing!
The sun is even bigger than
The biggest bonfire in the world.
The sun provides heat and light.
There are nine dazzling planets.
I live on the one and only Earth
I wonder if anything else is out there
Other than humans?
There is no gravity in space
So astronauts have to wear space suits mostly coloured white.
Space suits can protect them from flying dust that can hurt.
Asteroid fields can be dangerous to astronauts
Because they can shatter their rockets.
Space is almost pitch black.
It's ever lasting.
Space is the best.

Joshua Betts (8)
Woodland View Middle School

MY WINTER POEM

As the icicles fall off the trees
My feet begin to freeze.

The snow falls every day and night
Everything is covered in white.

I feel cold
As the sky goes bold.

As the breeze flows through the trees
I try to protect the bees.

Jenna Wales (9)
Woodland View Middle School

THE OLD ROBBER

The wind was a howling wolf sounding as if he would soon die,
The moon was a dormant, dark, dim face lodged up in the sky,
The road was a dusty ribbon next to the dark, old, deep moor,
And the soldier came riding -
Riding - riding
The soldier came riding up to the old castle door.

He wore a suit of gold armour and a black three-cornered hat,
He had a musket and a sword and was followed by a cat,
And on his feet he wore a pair of black polished leather boots,
A pair of gloves were on his hands,
From foreign lands,
On his horse there was a bag bulging full of loot.

He rode swiftly through the forest stirring up the leaves,
He was getting angry, as there was no treasure to be found,
He had searched the world for gold,
Now he was old,
He stopped, sighed and gave a groan, then fell dead on the ground.

Peter Cooper (9)
Woodland View Middle School

THE GHOST RIDER

The wind was a howling wolf racing round the bare, leafless trees,
The moon was a staring face tossed among the dark cloudy seas,
The road was a sparkling piece of ribbon twisting through the moors,
And the ghost-rider came riding -
Riding - riding -
The ghost-rider came riding up to the castle doors.

He'd a French cocked hat on his head and a pistol at his waist,
He moved silently towards the stables earnest in his haste,
He tied up his horse and called to someone in the dark shadows,
His love was ready and waiting -
Loving - waiting -
Together they left, making for the forest shadows.

They arrived in the forest, among the dark, shadowy trees,
They kissed by the light of the moonbeams and he fell to his knees,
'Be mine forever?' he asked his love, with pleading in his eye,
His lady was very happy -
Joyful - happy -
She smiled at him, her handsome man - 'Yes.' was her reply.

Suddenly they heard a gunshot and were surrounded by men,
'Quick love, get away and save yourself.' he shouted through the glen,
But the men, they did not stop to think and fired upon the pair,
And the couple lay there dying -
Bleeding - dying -
'Be mine forever.' he gasped - 'Yes.' breathed his lady fair.

Naomi Carpenter (10)
Woodland View Middle School

THE HIGHWAYMAN'S LOVE

The wind was a howling wolf running around the leafless trees,
The moon was a pale ghost kneeling down on its trembling knees,
The road was a slithering, shiny snake right under the shore,
And the highwayman came riding,
Riding, riding,
The highwayman came riding up to the old inn door.

He had a scar across his forehead, with sixteen stitches in,
He had a long red velvet coat and a lacy shirt within,
His horse has a beautiful jet black coat carrying on back man,
The highwayman came galloping,
Galloping, galloping,
And the highwayman came galloping as fast as he can.

In the spooky, gloomy dark inn everybody is sleeping,
The highwayman looked through the window ready to be peeping,
The highwayman took a quick flash into the landlord's bedroom,
He was killing the man quickly,
Quickly, quickly,
He killed the man quickly in the silver light of moon.

The highwayman runs to his horse where the landlord's daughter waits,
They both jump upon his horse, and gallop at a fast rate,
The relationship between the two of them is real true love,
There was kind twinkle,
Twinkle, twinkle,
There was a kind twinkle like in the eyes of a dove.

Lucy Mytton (9)
Woodland View Middle School

THE MUSKETEER

The wind was a howling wolf racing around the leafless trees,
The moon was a dim, dark diamond, far, far above the stormy seas,
The road was a whirling, winding path to the castle door
And the musketeer came galloping, galloping, the musketeer came
galloping up to the castle door.

He'd a French cocked hat upon his head, his long tailed coat was red,
'I shall have ze English King's head before I fall into bed.'
He laughed and laughed with evil glee for he was French through and
through,
He'd lost his hand in time of war,
(Oh it was sore!)
But still to his country he remained loyal and true.

He burst into the castle hall and raced towards the stairs.
The English soldiers, confused, cried out: 'To arms. Beware!'
A hundred gun shots echoed and re-echoed round the hall.
With screams and thuds many men fell, hearing deaths knell.
But the musketeer lay dying, pierced by many musket balls.

And still today French musketeers try to kill the English King,
But all they've managed to do so far is take his golden ring.
All those musketeers who have tried were brave, valiant and bold.
They carried out their duties well,
Though they all fell.
They lie forgotten in their graves, all lonely and cold.

Joe Wilcock (9)
Woodland View Middle School

AUTUMN

The wind is blowing
It howls through the trees
Growling like a lion
The animals are hibernating
In their cosy beds
The flowers are sleeping underground
The birds are flying south
Leaving their empty nests behind
I have to wear warm clothes.
Bonfire night!
The fires crackle
And the fireworks
Go bang!
Bright colours fill the air.
Hallowe'en!
The faces are scary
They give you a fright
Harvest!
The farmers are in the fields
Collecting vegetables
The weather!
It rains quite a lot
It's cold
Sometimes windy
Conker fights are fun
We throw leaves about
You have to wear coats
Smoke pours out of the chimney
Keeping people warm, not cold.
That's autumn!

Anna-Marie Watts (8)
Woodland View Middle School

WINTER

Slippery pavements
Icy roads
Cotton snow falling down
Snowball fights in the garden
Frosty cars on the road
Winter is a happy time
Big fat snowmen with a carrot nose
Doors creaking open
Presents under the tree
Snow carpets the garden
Everything bright with white
Winter is the best time
And that's what winter's like.

Adam Page (9)
Woodland View Middle School

WINTER

Winter brings us snow
Snowballs gushing down the hills
When you walk under the trees
Snowflakes fall on your head
Children snow fighting in the park
White grass instead of green
Crunchy, crispy leaves
Now the Millennium is here
People are getting presents.

Kelly Smith (9)
Woodland View Middle School

SPACE

Weird and wonderful
Space is expanding like a rubber band
Black as coal
Saturn and Uranus are fascinating
With bright rings around them.
Shooting stars like fireworks
Dazzle my eyes!
Neil Armstrong landed on the Moon
In 1969 in Apollo 11.
Grey and shiny Moon
Lights up the midnight sky.

John Fisher (9)
Woodland View Middle School

SPACE

Fiery dazzling sun high in the sky
Amazing sparkly shooting star
There are nine planets in the Milky Way
Big rockets zooming to the huge Moon
The smallest planet is Mars
The biggest is Jupiter
The Sun is our special star
Giving us heat and light
The sun is like a ball of fire
Glowing high in the sky

I think I would like to travel in space.

Daniel Grint (8)
Woodland View Middle School

TIN CAN MAN

I was walking down the street
When something shiny came along
Walking like a robot
Lonely and polite
As shiny as a crystal
With ring pulls for feet
And aluminium tufts of hair
A nose as long as a pointed needle
Ears as big as a pound coin
And a smiley happy red face
That used to have Dr Pepper in it
Until somebody drunk it all!
He's shaped like a cylinder
Bright and silvery in colour
Slowly he wanders down the street.

Sabrina Thompson (9)
Woodland View Middle School

WINTER

Icy roads
Soft snow is falling down
Slippery paths
Dead leaves scattered on the floor
Round and fat snowmen looking over us
Open new presents
Ice skating
Sledging down hills
It's all fantastic.

Bradley Garfield (8)
Woodland View Middle School

SPACE

Space is massive, black, full of stars!
Whooosh! Shooting stars go past me like fire
Saturn, Jupiter, Uranus, Neptune
Planets with diamond rings, Nature's miracles
Space is ever expanding
Venus, hundreds of miles away from us!
I want to travel to space
It's so fascinating, space is, so many planets to see
A meteor shower pelts an old satellite
Oh how I love its brilliance!
As the moon brightens at night it shines like a diamond.

Thomas Ryall (9)
Woodland View Middle School

THE SNAKE CHARMER

In the rain forest under the endless green canopy
Only a few creatures can be seen,
Making trips to the crystal clear water
Which is as cool as a butter dish.
In the dappled light a snake is bathing
Under the buttress roots of a thousand trees.
A bird is hidden at the top of the green enclosure
Warming itself under the life-giving sun,
Away from the hustle of a rain forest motorway
Carrying many animals through its green metropolis.

Matthew Dixon (10)
Woodland View Middle School

WE HAVE LIFT-OFF

5, 4, 3, 2, 1 we have lift-off,
I've got goosebumps, I'm worried,
I feel sick, it's bumpy too.
Finally I'm out in space,
It's cold, it's as black as ink.
I'm dancing,
I'm flying,
I'm singing too.
I start to whizz and whizz.
I'm bouncing, I'm whirling,
I see planets,
I see space too.
My boots are weighted,
But I can't feel them,
I see blue and the moon too,
But most of all I need the loo!

Jasmine Palmer (8)
Woodland View Middle School

WINTER

Winter brings white snow.
Ice, slippery on roads.
Snowballs
Made by cotton snow.
As snow falls
It freshens our minds.
Everywhere is cold
That's Christmas!

Phillip Fordham (9)
Woodland View Middle School

BESS MELRITHE

The wind was a howl from a wolf that was carried by the breeze.
The moon was a ship, being tossed upon the seven cloudy seas.
The road was a dusty, foggy, misty ribbon of moonlight.
And poor Bess Melrithe came riding -
Riding, riding,
Poor Bess Melrithe came riding up to the wood of fright.

She had long black hair that gleamed and shone in the stream of
moonlight.
She wore a long brown dress down to her ankle, that hid her from sight.
Her eyes were like sapphires gleaming and shining in the light.
Her lips were as red as roses -
Roses, roses,
She wore a cloak to hide the dress that hid her from sight.

As she approached, she saw him, a scary shadowy figure.
He had a horse and he wore a long, black cloak like her.
He held a big gun in one hand, and in the other a sword.
Yes, a shining sword and silver,
Silver, silver
He held the gun up high, she tossed her head in disorder.

It was King George's men, Kings George's men, poor, poor young girl
Bess.
He pulled the trigger, the bullet struck, and she fell, dead, poor Bess.
The gunpowder smoke filled the air, the wind blew strong, the smoke
was cleared.
Her face was pale, drained of her blood -
Red blood, red blood.
She lay dead, King George's men were now greatly feared.

Danielle Cawdron (9)
Woodland View Middle School

THE SNAKE CHARMER

Away in the darkness,
on the highest perch
sits an elegant bird
watching over the forest.
Down by the riverbed,
a shadowy figure,
stands alone playing the flute.
Along comes a magical bird
to watch the figure play.
From the depths of the forest
comes a rustling,
and above the shadowed figure
comes a snake, a grand snake flying over
branches
dancing to the sound of the flute,
from the rustling came other snakes
grand snakes, even grander than the first.
The mysterious figure picks a snake up
and places it around its neck.
The trees rustle in the wind,
moonlight shines through the forest canopy.
The music from the flute calms every snake.
All is peaceful in the forest,
with the sound of such soothing music.
The sky is a red and green colour,
the humidity makes the place like a jungle
The music still plays
but now seeming to travel away.

The snakes follow the sound until
it no longer plays.
But still everything is peaceful
as the mysterious figure disappears
into the darkest depths of the forest.

Michael Burroughs (10)
Woodland View Middle School

THE ROCKING HORSE

Outside the rocking horse the glistening paintwork
Sparkles as a loose ray of sun happens to catch it
Through the crack in the window.
The deep black eyes come to life and tell a story
Of the tragedy it has survived.

Inside the rocking horse live the pictures of what has happened,
The neglect, the painful feelings of being forgotten.
Left in this ruined nursery,
Haunted by the memories of that night,
That night of awfulness
Seeing the house destroyed by fire.

Its dreams are those of hope,
Hope to be found and played with again,
To hear the youngsters laugh with glee.
The longing for this pleasure will live with him for ever,
Now the only one to rock him is the breeze
That occasionally comes through that crack in the window.

Amy Platten (11)
Woodland View Middle School

UP, UP AND AWAY

I went to a space station
a spaceship was free
so I hopped in
up, up and away
galaxies far away
aliens green and slimy
red hot, blue cold
different shapes and colours.

'Apollo 13,' I read
we started to speed
one hot sizzling sun.

Hot, I woke up
hot, I left my blanket on
next day I went and will go
up, up and away
every day
help, hot, help, my dreams!

Lynsey South (9)
Woodland View Middle School

UP, UP AND AWAY

Up, up and away,
I went away today,
Up in the clouds, up in the sky,
The best bit of this is to fly.

Up, up and away,
I went away today,
Up in the heavens, up in the snow,
As the rivers go by, they flow.

Up, up and away,
I went away today,
One of the people fainted, *flop!*
Oh no, a plane! *Pop!*

Luke Nolan Goffin (9)
Woodland View Middle School

THE GHOST RIDER

The wind was a howling monster blowing like a black tie,
The moon was a staring face up high in the cloudless black sky,
The road was a slithering, slimy worm crawling on the floor,
and the ghost rider came riding - riding - riding -
The ghost rider came riding up to the castle door.

He wore a bright blue kilt with a gold and silver handled sword,
When he came through the big wooden castle door he roared,
He picked up his wife, Tess, and rode away on the dusty mess,
He rode away on the highway,
He rode away,
And he rode away on the highway with his wife, Tess.

But then came a ghost catcher and shot down Tess with one shot,
He jumped up and charged away quickly on the dot,
He galloped away to the castle and came into a room
And there he lay alone, himself, and on the shelf,
Was a picture of Tess who he know was in eternal doom.

The next morning, up he got and went to find the killer,
He found on the highway his loved one, Tess, it might be a miller,
But then he came across a soldier, it was he who was the killer,
And shot the ghost rider, right beside her,
And there was a mill across the road and out came the miller.

Matthew Robson (10)
Woodland View Middle School

THE BIG SMUGGLER

The wind was a calm sea; a calm wind was blowing across the sky.
The moon was a faded colour in the blue high dusky sky,
The road was a wiggly worm squirming over a big brown broom,
And the big smuggler came riding -
Riding, riding -
The big smuggler came riding up to the storage room.

His black coat was made of a fine bit of lace, his coat was sweaty.
His horses were getting hungry, they stopped for some spaghetti.
His hat was a dark red, so people couldn't see him very well,
His cloak was covering his face.
He had a base.
The road in front of him was dim, it was like dark hell.

His lover was awaiting by a shimmering canal.
On the other side of the water, was his trusty pal.
The big smuggler found his lover and they started talking,
He told her not to look round the bend.
Don't tell your friend,
Don't tell your friend, it is important, just keep walking.

We've nearly finished our job, so there's no need to tell anyone.
Don't tell anyone, because our job is almost over and done,
All we have to do is get the rum in the storage room.
We've collected rum and beer,
Also deer.
The job is done and finished, so we all shout . . . *Kaboom!*

Daniel Norrish (9)
Woodland View Middle School

ANIMALS IN CAPTIVITY - TIGERS

The unhappy tigers roam all day,
Thinking of where they used to be.
Where has all their freedom gone?
Wishing of bathing under the sun.
The miserable hunters 'Where's my prey?'
Roaming around unhappy all day.

Where they used to be,
Oh I hate tigers in captivity.

Most of the tigers are being used,
Why can't they bathe in the muddy pools?
Circuses allow this disgraceful thing to happen,
And why do you have to capture them?

Where they used to be,
Oh I hate tigers in captivity.

Gloomy inside their eyes you can see,
Their gloominess of captivity.
Warmth, moonlight and the sun,
Why can't they have any fun?

Where they used to be,
Oh I hate tigers in captivity.

Cara Oxbury (9)
Woodland View Middle School

THE WHALER

The wind was a coiling rope twisting around the leafless trees,
The moon was a pale coin drifting upon silent and still seas,
The road was a shimmering, silver snake on the cobbled ground,
And King George's men came riding,
Riding, riding,
The red coats came riding up to the high cliff top mound.

The whaler in tawdry, tawny garments called upon rough seas,
La Morte Baleine the whaler's ship swayed on an uneasy breeze,
The whaler stepped aboard his ship he was prepared and so keen,
The ship set forth over the waves,
Drifting on waves,
Red coats followed whaler's ship, none of them could be seen.

The red coats sailed a steady path upon the sea so dark blue,
The red coats sailed for weeks and weeks their determination grew,
They fired twice using a cannon second time lucky they hit,
Down slowly down,
The whaler though had swum right up, he was well and fit.

The whaler swam to a shore so distant he was never found,
He roamed around searching for shelter he found some
modest ground,
He built himself a wooden hut from where trees around him lay,
He lived a peaceful life and then,
While in his den,
An arrow in the head from a monster one dismal day.

Elspeth Clayton (10)
Woodland View Middle School

THE SMUGGLERS

The wind was fierce, the smugglers on horseback made for the road
The moon shone, they piled the goods high, horses bent under the load
The road was long and narrow, it lead to their dark spooky cave
And the smugglers went trotting
Trotting, trotting,
And the smugglers kept trotting, they were very brave.

They ran down the beach, got in their boat, by now they were so cold
They set sail to sea with a row-boat full of brandy and gold
Spray hit their faces, coats were sodden, one more mile to the cave
And the smugglers kept rowing
Rowing, rowing
At last they were done, they parted with smiles and a wave.

Matthew Singleton (9)
Woodland View Middle School

UP, UP AND AWAY

A   eroplanes go up in the sky,
E   at, eating, time for tea,
R   oar, roar goes the rocket taking off,
O   ver the clouds, over the sea,
P   eople small, buildings tall,
L   eaving from the land below,
A   way, away goes everything,
N   ight comes, night goes,
E   ven time ticks as I go by,
S   ky, sky, I am in the sky.

Claudia Emily Roe (10)
Woodland View Middle School

Up, Up And Away

As I fly through the air,
With the wind in my hair,
I hold on tight
With all my might.
I pass some trees
Swaying in the breeze.
Higher and higher and higher I go,
More and more the wind does blow
Faster and faster I go
Up here it's beginning to snow
Up, up and away.
Can I get back by the end of the day?
Will this balloon ever stop?
Oh no . . . ! A plane . . . ! *Pop!*

Paul Judge (9)
Woodland View Middle School

Up, Up And Away

We're going on an aeroplane
On a holiday to Spain.
We've checked in with our passports
We're getting on the plane.

We're going up the runway
Then taking off
My brother keeps saying, 'Up, up and away.'
My ears have gone funny.

We're going over mountains
The houses look like dots.
We go through fluffy clouds
It looks just like fog.

We're landing on the runway
The wheels hit the ground
We're getting off the plane
We're in Spain.

Katie Barnes (10)
Woodland View Middle School

UP, UP AND AWAY

Up, up and away,
Another day,
Right away in the sky.
It's nice to fly,
Among the clouds,
And the birds make crowds,
Up, up and away.

The trees freeze,
In the cold, cold breeze,
A very thick fog,
A cloud like a hog,
Am I in a train?
No, I'm in a plane,
Up, up and away.

Richard Castle (9)
Woodland View Middle School

Up, Up And Away

I'm flying in a helicopter
And I crash into a plane,
Oh no, what a shame.
I fly past all the birds,
I'm flying on a magic carpet
Gliding through the air,
And give all the birds
A terrific scare.
I'm in a hot air balloon,
Floating over the sea,
Oh no, I'm late for tea.
I'm gliding up to space,
I'm on a mission
I'm on the case,
I've just come down and crashed,
But I'll go back up, up and away!

Laura Katie Brancalion (9)
Woodland View Middle School